H. S. BENNETT

SIX MEDIEVAL MEN AND WOMEN

CAMBRIDGE
At the University Press
1955

CAMBRIDGE UNIVERSITY PRESS
Cambridge, New York, Melbourne, Madrid, Cape Town,
Singapore, São Paulo, Delhi, Mexico City

Cambridge University Press
The Edinburgh Building, Cambridge CB2 8RU, UK

Published in the United States of America by Cambridge University Press, New York

www.cambridge.org
Information on this title: www.cambridge.org/9781107685772

First published 1955
First paperback edition 2013

A catalogue record for this publication is available from the British Library

ISBN 978-1-107-68577-2 Paperback

To

JANET AND GEORGE TREVELYAN

WITH

GRATITUDE AND AFFECTION

CONTENTS

PREFACE

In his inaugural lecture at Cambridge as Regius Professor of Modern History, Professor Knowles remarked that 'academic historians are notably less concerned with men and women, their personalities and their characters, than they were a century ago. If Charles Kingsley's saying, that "History is the history of men and women, and nothing else", seemed paradoxical in his own day, it would seem scandalous now.' But what may seem 'scandalous' in the eyes of a professional historian may yet have its attractions for that large body of readers with historical curiosity, to whom the spectacle of men and women 'doing things' can never be without interest, and it is for them that this book is written. It sets out to give an account of the lives of a few men and women of the fifteenth century, hoping that it will enable the modern reader to understand something of what it meant to be a soldier or a civil servant, or the wife of a country land-owner at that time. In the background are the wars in France and the unrest at home, but these are considered only in so far as they are necessary for an understanding of the narrative.

This volume incorporates the substance of the Gregynog Lectures delivered at the University College of

Wales, Aberystwyth, during the Session 1952–3, and I gratefully record the honour done me, and the gracious hospitality shown to me while I was there. Since then I have revised and enlarged the lectures extensively, and some of them have been given on the Alexander White foundation at the University of Chicago in the Spring Quarter of 1955. Here again I can only express my obligation for the many kindnesses I received on my fourth visit to this great university of the Middle West.

H. S. B.

EMMANUEL COLLEGE,
CAMBRIDGE

HUMPHREY, DUKE OF GLOUCESTER

In August 1390, Henry, earl of Derby, the eldest son of John of Gaunt, joined the army of the Teutonic Order, in response to an invitation by the grand master, inviting knights of all nations to take part in a military expedition against the heathen Lithuanians on the north-east border of Germany. The Order had for centuries been active in propagating Christianity by fire and by sword, and frequently during the past fifty years had been on warlike terms with their neighbours in Lithuania. Henry joined the main forces of the army on 22 August and from then on, with his knights and retainers to the number of about two hundred, took part in many skirmishes and battles until the attackers were held up outside the Lithuanian capital of Wilna. Although they won some partial success, after about five weeks of indecisive fighting, with autumn approaching, sickness in their midst and rations running out, they retired, and Henry set up his quarters for the winter at Königsberg. It was there, during the first few days of November, that a sailor brought Henry the news of the birth of his fourth son which had taken place a month or so earlier. The earl gave the sailor a mark (13*s.* 4*d.*) for his pains—the equivalent of six or seven weeks' pay.

Henry, of course, as the eldest son of John of Gaunt, was wealthy and had great expectations, while his wife was a co-heiress of Humphrey de Bohun and owner of vast estates. Their fourth son was named Humphrey in memory of his grandfather. Thus descended from two of the richest and most powerful families in England, the young boy's prospects were favourable indeed. Presumably he was brought up in such a fashion as befitted his position, living with his brothers and sisters on various family estates, mostly in the west country. His mother died when he was only four years old, so that he was left in the care of a nurse, who in turn was succeeded by a governess, and later by a master. Such domestic accounts as survive are not very revealing. They record the purchase of kirtles, shoes, robes, etc., for his use, while for special occasions—as on the death of his grandfather—a black livery was bought for him, just as on a more festive occasion he was decked out with a scarlet gown and cap. The most splendid of these events was the coming of his new 'mother'—the second wife of Henry. Humphrey was taken to London for the marriage, and he and his brother presented the bride—Joan of Navarre—with a splendid pair of gold tablets, bought from a London goldsmith for the considerable sum of £79.

All this made little difference to the young boy, who was only just beginning to learn the elementary duties and responsibilities of his rank when the whole family position was suddenly altered. On the death of John of Gaunt, Humphrey's father returned from the exile imposed on him in 1398 by Richard II, and after a short while in England, seized Richard, 'challenged for the crown', and on 30 September 1399, ascended the throne as Henry IV.

Despite this dramatic change Humphrey appears to have grown up with no more than the usual rewards and emoluments coming his way as the youngest son of the king. Lands, dignities and offices enhanced his position, but do not seem to have brought him into the main current of national affairs, and it was not until his brother ascended the throne as Henry V in 1413 that steps were taken to bring him out of the quiet, inconspicuous world which he inhabited so that he might play his part in the high matters of State which were by then calling for attention.

As a prelude to this he was created earl of Pembroke and duke of Gloucester in 1414, an action which gave him a high place in the peerage, and enabled him to command respect as he took his place in the anxious councils which at that time were being held while the question of our future action against France was debated. The moment was a decisive one, for France was divided, and the time seemed ripe for the English to ally themselves with one of the contending parties, and so win a dominating position in French affairs.

English opinion was far from united as to which party would best serve our interests as an ally. Henry V, together with many powerful nobles, leaned towards the party headed by the powerful duke of Burgundy. Their rivals, the Armagnacs (as the followers of the house of Orleans were called), seemed the better choice to Humphrey and his brother Clarence, as it had seemed in earlier years to their father. What was behind Humphrey's view is unknown, but it is of interest to note that even as a tyro in politics he should have taken his own line—a line to which he adhered throughout his life. To him Burgundy was always the enemy.

As the debate went forward throughout 1414 and the early months of 1415, Gloucester, like many others, must have known that there was but little reality in it for the most part, since neither of the French parties could possibly have accepted Henry's foremost demand for the crown of France. Nor could Gloucester have been unaware that these negotiations barely hid Henry's growing determination to invade France with fire and sword if need be. At length the moment all were waiting for came; and, after hectic weeks of preparation in England, Humphrey found himself one of a large invading force which landed in France in mid-August 1415.

He had everything to learn. Although he is said to have been present at the battle of Shrewsbury in 1403, it is unlikely that a boy of twelve took part in the battle itself. Now, a man of twenty-four, he began his apprenticeship at the wars. To begin with the English found their passage up the Seine valley barred by the garrison of the fortified town of Harfleur, so that several weeks of siege operations were necessary before it fell. Gloucester was posted on the west side of the town and given charge of the cannons used to bombard the walls and barbicans. The besieged were given no rest: day by day the heavy missiles made breaches in the walls which could only be partially repaired by night. Attacked not only on the west, but also on the east by Clarence's forces, after five weeks the defenders were forced to surrender. (For a more detailed account of this campaign, see p. 40.)

This was the first of many sieges in which Humphrey was to take a leading part during the next few years. It is true that his brother is said to have put him where the fight was fiercest at Harfleur, and later to have given him command of a squadron at Agincourt, where he was said to have displayed conspicuous—almost reckless—courage, but it was as a director of siege artillery that his reputation grew. He obviously had studied to good effect the medieval treatises on the subject, and wherever he was in charge, his ability, combined with his disregard of danger, generally saw the English forces victorious. By the end of the 1415–20 campaigns, Gloucester had seen service far and wide in Upper and Lower Normandy, and was renowned as a gifted and resourceful conductor of artillery sieges. He had had little experience as a strategist, or as a commander on a large scale, but what he had done had often been so remarkable and successful that he was looked on by many as one of the outstanding soldiers of his day.

His most spectacular feat was the subjection of Cherbourg in 1418. Froissart once described the castle on its northern side as the strongest in the world. It stood within the formidable town walls, which were lapped by the high tide, while deep ditches on the southern side of the town made it seem wellnigh impregnable. To the west the country was water-logged, with shifting sandy soil which gave the besiegers no help, and as they tried to build up more solid foundations from which to attack, the French set fire to the brush and faggots painfully hauled into place to be used as a shelter from which to attack. Flaming tow, claws flung out from the walls and volleys of cannon-balls made the lot of the English an unenviable one, and it was not long before Gloucester changed his tactics, and prepared to starve the garrison into submission. His main force was withdrawn out of the enemy's range, forward towers and protective ditches were made, while from time to time a variety of attempts to find a weak spot in the French defences kept everyone busy, as huge digging operations threw up great mounds from which it was hoped to scale the battlements and the sappers burrowed their way forward, only to be defeated by the rock and treacherous sand which confronted them. On their side the French were unable to do more than keep the enemy at bay by constant cannon fire and the use of catapult and other engines of war. They harried the besiegers at every turn, but were so closely invested that they knew that unless help came it was only a matter of time before they would be forced to capitulate. No help did come; on the contrary, Gloucester was heavily reinforced by sea in the late summer, and finally the five-month siege came to an end at Michaelmas, and Gloucester and his men were free to join the king at Rouen, where they were given a post of honour in the great operations which resulted in the surrender of the town in January 1419. Gloucester was active in France throughout this year, but his days as a commander were numbered, and although he saw more service, he was never again to take so active or so honourable a part in the wars between England and France.

As a first sign of a change of direction in his activities, we find that on 30 December 1419, he was appointed 'guardian and lieutenant of England', in place of his brother Bedford, whose advice was urgently required in France in the negotiations which led to the treaty of Troyes, the marriage of the French king's daughter, Catherine, to Henry, and the end of another phase of the Hundred Years War. Henceforth, Gloucester's main place was at the council table, or in the intervals of business in his library, for he was already showing signs of an interest in books which in the event was to be his chief title to fame. Hoccleve, about this time, says of him that:

> Next our lord lige, our kyng victorious,
> In al this wyde world, lord is ther noon,
> Un-to me so good ne so gracious
> And haath been swich, yeeres ful many oon.

The exchange of offices cannot have been altogether to his taste, for he found he had but limited power. He could only act 'with the assent of and after deliberation by the Council, and not otherwise', and in any case, the thoughts and energies of England were overseas, so that not much of importance was happening at home at that time.

It was not until the death of Henry V that the real test came. On his death-bed in France, the king had expressed his desire that Gloucester should act as Regent in England for the infant Henry VI while Bedford was acting as Regent in France. The difficulties facing Gloucester were considerable: the problems which were bound to arise from the long minority of the boy king had to be met without the powerful leadership of the sagacious Bedford, and under the critical eye, and often with the violent opposition of Henry Beaufort, bishop of Winchester.

A legitimized bastard of the royal blood, Beaufort had shown much ability and energy in various great positions, such as Lord Chancellor, and had deep practical knowledge of current politics, for there was more of the politician and man of affairs than of the churchman about him. His knowledge, his family connexions, his high office in Church and State and his immense riches made him an outstanding figure, so that it was almost inevitable that a clash for power between him and Gloucester would develop. It did, and for more than twenty years the enmity of these two men is a recurrent motif in the story of English statecraft.

The death of Henry V gave Beaufort his chance to gain power and he was quick to take it. Gloucester's claims as Regent were strictly scrutinized by the Council (dominated by the Beaufort faction as it was) and many of them denied or limited in scope. Gloucester found that his wings were clipped. The Bishop and his friends hedged him in; and, to a man of Gloucester's impetuous temperament, this state of affairs was a constant incentive to mischief-making and encouraged qualities of intrigue and political manœuvre in the Prince which brought out the worst sides of his nature. He was forced to rely upon one expedient after another, and found himself clutching at this or that political device in order to gain time or to win a temporary advantage. He was no more of a strategist at home than he had been in the field: his genius was not for long-term politics and this combined with his nervous temperament often gave his opponents the advantage. Slowly Beaufort wore him down: a long series of encounters between the two resulted at times in a temporary advantage for Gloucester, but Beaufort generally took the long view, and made peace with his opponent when that seemed best. By caution, ceaseless diplomacy and his prestige, however, he gradually swung the balance in his own favour, and by 1430 undoubtedly had the upper hand and steadily outmanœuvred the duke at most points.

But Gloucester was always powerful until nearly the end, in part because of his high position as the king's uncle, and for some years next in succession to the throne, and in part because of the special place he held in the hearts and affections of the ordinary people—in particular the citizens of London. Early in life 'the good duke', as they loved to call him, had won the enthusiastic loyalty of the Londoners, and they were a great source of support to him throughout. The growing demands of the middle-class townsmen were understood by him and he was active on their behalf from time to time. In domestic affairs generally he was a firm ruler: lawlessness found in him a severe and energetic opponent who was always ready to appear in person wherever there was trouble, and would stamp out revolt with a peremptory authority. Unorthodoxy in matters of religion he treated with great severity, and was ever a faithful son of Holy Church, especially generous to his beloved abbey of St Albans.

But much more than domestic policy was involved in the career of Gloucester. The war in France was continuously requiring attention. Money, men, munitions were drained away in a seemingly unending series of campaigns. The loss of leaders such as Talbot, and later of Bedford himself; the victories of Joan of Arc; the constant intrigues with this or that French faction—all presented problems which would not wait for an answer. And Gloucester had only one answer—war. From the moment he was brought into public affairs to the end, his attitude was uncompromising. The House of Burgundy, in particular called forth his implacable hostility; but, Burgundian or Armagnac, he steadily advocated a policy of no compromise. This unyielding attitude constantly put him in the wrong at the Council table, although it almost certainly increased his popularity with the ordinary people. His senseless obstinacy in the face of changing conditions reflects badly upon his reputation as a statesman. Thus, when in 1438 our position in France after the death of Bedford had seriously deteriorated and *pourparlers* for peace were opened, Gloucester would have none of it. He opposed any peace policy; he violently objected to the release of the duke of Orleans, who had been in honourable captivity ever since Agincourt. Beaufort and others thought his return to France would be a help in making a peace between the two countries, but Gloucester believed it would be inimical to our interests, and publicly registered his protest by walking out during the ceremony in which Orleans swore never again to fight against England. Henceforward Gloucester's part in foreign affairs was but small. His opponents had the upper hand, and at this moment (1441) a most untoward event in his family life put him even further at their mercy. We must now go back many years to trace the tangled skeins in Gloucester's private life which brought this about.

In the intervals of politics and soldiering Gloucester was indulging in his two passions—love and books. Pius II once declared that the duke was a man more suited to a life of lust and of letters than to one of arms, and his actions certainly gave some justification to the charge. The fifteenth century was far from being an age of scrupulous morals, but Humphrey's conduct was notorious. By the time he was thirty-five things were so serious with him that his personal physician had warned him against the consequences of his excesses, and an anonymous chronicle declared that the duke 'excelled all the princes of the world in knowledge, in comeliness of appearance, and in fame, but he possessed an unbalanced mind, was effeminate and given over to sensual pleasures, a tendency which vitiated all his actions'.

It was perhaps for these reasons that he delayed marrying until a comparatively late age for a man of his time and position, since it was only in 1422, at the age of thirty-two, that he married Jacqueline of Bavaria, daughter of William IV, Count of Hainault, Holland and Zeeland. She had been twice previously married, but had quarrelled bitterly with her second husband, John of Brabant, over the disposal of her territory for a period to John of Bavaria, and in desperation fled to England in April 1421. As Warden of the Cinque Ports it was Humphrey's duty to receive this twenty-year-old girl at Dover and to escort her to his brother Henry V at Westminster. Jacqueline was only a pawn in Henry's continental policy, whether as a help in his transactions with Burgundy or in other ways is not clear, but for that reason she was made very welcome, and given the handsome allowance of £100 a month while resident in England.

Before long it was clear that Humphrey was interested in this guest of his brother, but his advances were postponed for a time since he was absent in France throughout the rest of 1421, and only returned to England early in 1422. Matters quickly ripened between the two, and despite the fact that her marriage to John of Brabant was but dubiously dissolved, according to some authorities, Gloucester married her probably in September or October of that year. What was it that attracted this handsome experienced roué to Jacqueline? Certainly not her beauty if contemporary portraits do not belie her. Perhaps her imperious, passionate temperament appealed to him, but the likelihood is (as early historians asserted) that it was her inheritance which attracted him. As we know, Gloucester was violently opposed to Burgundy, and the fact that Jacqueline's possessions were being handed over to John of Bavaria, one of Burgundy's followers, certainly gave an added zest to his wooing, since neither Jacqueline nor Gloucester was unwilling to risk a trial of strength with Burgundy. Not that this seemed inevitable at this time, for Gloucester's brother Bedford had but recently married Anne, sister of Philip of Burgundy. It was not long, however, before Bedford became aware of the dangers attending his brother's schemes to retain Jacqueline's possessions, since Burgundy was equally determined to get control of them. Despite various attempts by Bedford to bring about an agreement between the two parties Gloucester was determined to assert his right to control his wife's territories, and in October 1424 crossed with her to Calais, attended by a force of about 4000 horse and foot, and invaded Hainault. If Gloucester hoped to be welcomed as a saviour he was disappointed. The burghers little relished this overbearing foreigner or his pretentions. They recognized him only as the husband of their countess, and grudgingly raised the funds that he demanded. His army was detested since Humphrey failed to control its raids and exactions. The news that Burgundy was in arms against the invader soon proved to be true; his troops crossed the border and a series of indecisive skirmishes took place in which Gloucester's tactics and leadership were poor.

Meanwhile a series of letters was passing between Burgundy and Gloucester, in the course of which Burgundy asserted that Gloucester had called him a liar, and therefore he challenged Gloucester to a duel. The challenge was accepted and Burgundy began to train for the combat. Such an event would not easily have been allowed, however; Bedford did all he could to avert the duel and a papal bull sternly denounced any such happening. Finally, a conference between representatives of both parties declared that neither principal had any reason to proceed to such extremities, and the matter was dropped.

Gloucester was probably relieved, for he had for some months been in a different mood from his early days in Hainault. He was mortified and disheartened by the tepid welcome that he had received there, and was becoming increasingly aware of the difficulties he had created for himself and for his country by his wanton defiance of Burgundy. His zeal for his wife's cause waned as quickly as it had been ignited, and on the pretext of preparing for his duel with Burgundy and of the need of his presence in England on urgent affairs about mid-April he had left Hainault, never to return. Jacqueline accompanied him for the first few miles, and then returned to face the ever growing Burgundian menace alone.

All this shows Gloucester in a poor enough light, but worse remains to be told. Although he wrote from Calais promising Jacqueline that he would soon be back, he had, in fact, turned his affections elsewhere. 'Dame Jacque la désirée', as she was sometimes called, had in her train a certain Madame de Warigny, and it looks as if she entertained Gloucester for part of his sojourn in Hainault. But if so, his attentions were but fleeting, for among the ladies-in-waiting brought from England was Eleanor

Cobham, 'a handsome, greedy, sensual woman of doubtful antecedents'. Soon after the duke's return to England, it was common gossip that she was his mistress. Henceforth, Jacqueline meant less and less. She wrote him pathetic letters, saying that 'all my hopes and expectations are in your control; you are my only and sovereign joy and all that I suffer is from love of you'. She goes on: 'I implore you humbly and as tenderly as one can in this world, that for God's sake you may have pity on me and my misery and come to aid me, your forlorn creature, as speedily as possible, if you do not wish to lose me for ever. I hope that you will do this.... Yes, I am ready at any moment to encounter death from love of you, for your lordship is all my delight.'

All in vain. Gloucester paid but perfunctory attention to affairs in Hainault, even though for a time Jacqueline was a prisoner of Burgundy. She escaped, and Gloucester sent a small force to her aid early in 1426. This availed nothing, for Burgundy decisively defeated this body as well as Jacqueline's scanty levies. Undismayed, the countess continued to oppose Burgundy wherever she could find support, and in April 1427 appealed to the Council of England—not to Humphrey—for help. Further urgent letters persuaded the Council to grant money for an expedition to furnish garrison troops for places which remained faithful to Jacqueline and to bring her to England. The risks of becoming embroiled with Burgundy inherent in such a plan were obvious, and Bedford brought all his influence to bear on Gloucester and Burgundy, and patched up a truce between them late in 1427.

Meanwhile, in January 1428, the pope at last decided that

Jacqueline's marriage with the Duke of Brabant was valid, and as a consequence that between her and Gloucester invalid. This was the end. Gloucester was free, and any question of another expedition to Hainault was no longer practical politics. Despite political considerations, however, the human relation between the two persons led the mayor and aldermen of London to protest, and offer financial support for the helping of Jacqueline. The women of London went further, and in the most public fashion gave letters to various lords, protesting against the duke's action in abandoning Jacqueline for the harlot Eleanor. All was of no avail. Jacqueline passed out of his life and Gloucester hastened to marry Eleanor. The chronicler Hall, a hundred years later, thus sums up Gloucester's position: 'if he wer unquieted with his other pretensed wife, truly he was tenne tymes more vexed by occasion of this woman—so that he began his marriage with evill, and ended it with worse.'

In writing thus Hall refers to the great scandal that broke about the duke in 1441 when his wife was accused of practising necromancy and the black arts. The years between their marriage and her disgrace tell us next to nothing of their life together. There were no children born after their marriage, although rumour credited them with two before this, and the few mentions of Eleanor see her receiving the robes of the Garter, or grants of land, much as would be expected to fall to a woman of her station. By 1441 Gloucester's authority in the State was wellnigh ended, but some historians believe his enemies used the charge against his wife to deliver the *coup de grâce*. As a preliminary, charges were brought against two men, Roger Bolingbroke, an Oxford priest, 'a great and cunning man in astronomy', and Thomas Southwell, canon of St Stephen's, Westminster, who were accused of making a wax image of Henry VI, which they exposed to a slow fire, and by aid of the devil, as the image melted, so the life of the king would fade away. Bolingbroke, on a July Sunday in 1441, was placed on a high scaffold outside St Paul's, arrayed in his magic garments. About him were the writings, the images of wax, silver and metal, together with other instruments of his craft. He had a paper crown and there before the multitude swore to abuse his false craft of the devil. From there he was taken to the Tower to await further judgement.

A few days later rumour had it that he had acted at the instigation of Eleanor, who had asked him to use his arts to determine 'to what estate in life she should come', and presumably to prepare the wax image. Whatever truth there was in the matter, Eleanor took fright and ran for sanctuary at Westminster. This availed her little, for the right of sanctuary could not protect her from charges of heresy and witchcraft, treason and necromancy which the Church formulated against her, and she took to the river in an attempt to escape, but was taken and brought before her judges, where Bolingbroke testified against her. The usual delays followed, and while Eleanor vigorously denied a number of charges, nevertheless she 'submitted to the correction of the Bishops', abjured her heresies and witchcraft and appeared before them for sentence early in November. Here she was ordered to do penance in the most public manner, which her exalted rank made only the more conspicuous. On three days it was decreed that she was to be brought by barge from Westminster to the

City. On the first of these, a Monday, she was met at the steps of Temple Bridge by the mayor, sheriffs and notables of the City gilds who accompanied her on her penitential progress through the crowds lining Fleet Street and Ludgate Hill. As she passed them they saw that she was bare-footed with her hood drawn back, so that all could see her face clearly. On she went, until she reached St Paul's, and there at the high altar made offering of the large candle of two pounds' weight which she had carried in her hand all the way. On Wednesday she landed at the Swan in Thames Street and went in similar fashion to Christchurch, Aldgate, whilst on the Friday her route lay between Queenhithe and up Cheapside to St Michael's, Cornhill.

After this she was given in charge to Sir Thomas Stanley, and began her eighteen years' imprisonment in one castle after another far from London and the scenes of her many triumphs. So 'Eleanor, lately called Duchess of Gloucester', as she is henceforth styled, passes; and the manner of her passing, her pride and her high station made a great impression on all at that time. The chroniclers record the whole episode with unusual fullness, and a contemporary poem, *The Lament of the Duchess of Gloucester*, puts into verse what must have been the half-formed thoughts of many:

In worldly joy and worthynes
  I was besette on every side;
Of Glowcestere I was duches,
  Amonge alle women magnyfyed.
As Lucyfer felle down for pryde,
  I felle from alle felycyté:
I hade no grace my self to gyde;
  Alle women may be ware by me.

Farewelle, London, and have good day;
  At thee I take my leve this tyde.
Farewelle, Grenwych, for ever and ay;
  Farewelle, fayre places on Temmys syde;
Farewelle, alle welthe and the world so wide.
  I am assigned where I shall be;
Under mens kepyng I must abide.
  Alle women may be ware by me.

Farewelle, my mynstrels, and alle your songe,
  That ofte hath made me for to daunce.
Farewelle; I wott I have done wronge;
  And I wyte my mysgovernaunce.
Now I lyste nother to pryke nor praunce;
  My pryde ys put to poverté.
Thus, both in Englond and in Fraunce,
  Alle women may be ware by me.

Meanwhile, Gloucester was powerless. It may well be that he realized that his enemies were striking at him through the duchess, and striking at a point where he was certainly vulnerable, for his own known interest in astrology and in astrological writings might easily have given his opponents a splendid opportunity had he shown any fight. No wonder that, as the chronicler says, he 'took all things patiently and said little'. With both churchmen and politicians united in their outlook on this matter, silence was best.

His life was rapidly running out. At his great manor house of 'Plaisance' at Greenwich, which he had so lavishly constructed, or at one of his many other manors, he lived in semi-retirement. In 1442 he pressed for an Armagnac marriage in opposition to Beaufort's scheme to marry the young king to Margaret of Anjou, and once again he was defeated. It was the final blow to any hopes he might have still nourished of any political future, for Margaret was hand in glove with Beaufort and his supporters, and their policy was inevitably one inimical to Gloucester's interests. Once the decision had been made, however, Gloucester capitulated and headed the impressive escort sent to welcome Margaret on her arrival in England. With a guard of honour of 500 men, all dressed in his livery, Gloucester rode with the queen after her marriage to Titchfield Abbey. All this did him no good, however. The months that followed showed that his opponents were determined to isolate him from any effective part in public affairs, and men openly said that his day was over. All that was left was the one great passion of his life—his library and his love of learning.

'You have no real pleasure, apart from the reading of books', wrote one of his followers, and although this is obviously an exaggeration, it has much truth in it. His popular title, 'the good duke', derives in part from his patronage of learning. Before he was thirty he was well known as a benefactor of writers. Hoccleve tells us that the duke has been good and gracious to him for many years, while Lydgate wrote one of his most voluminous works at the express wish of Gloucester.

We may with reason think of him in the 1420's as occupying his leisure in reading and collecting books in manuscript. From what we know of his library it is likely that during the first part of his career as a collector he was acquiring books that fell into certain well-known classes. Theology, naturally has a considerable place. 'The queen of sciences' could not be ignored by any cultivated layman, but it has been pointed out that 'the theology of Humphrey's library betrays a tendency to ignore medieval doctrinaires, and to turn to the early Fathers, who wrote before imperial Rome had passed into final decay'. Law, which might have been expected to form a considerable section of the library of one so much concerned with statecraft, is almost ignored. Books of both canon and civil law are few. The practical administrator in Humphrey found more nourishment in the standard works of history, the reading of which was thought by men of the time to serve as a stimulus to heroic action and noble ideas. Among ancient historians he had the works of Suetonius and Josephus; from medieval times those of Eusebius, Vincent of Beauvais, Bede and Higden.

So far his library was one which any well-read collector might have acquired. The particular interests of Humphrey are shown when we turn to see the great number of volumes on astronomy and astrology that he possessed. The works of the leading authorities in these abstruse and potentially dangerous arts are well represented, and together with his medical books form an outstanding section of his library. Humphrey showed the keenest interest in medical matters, and the authorities, ancient and modern, were all to be found on his shelves.

Furthermore, from the scattered remnants of his library, and from contemporary references, we can see how widely he cast his net. Both classical and contemporary literature delighted him. Ovid, Terence and Seneca; the works of Boccaccio, Petrarch and Dante; contemporary English and French writers—all found a place on his shelves. Were this all, however, Gloucester's fame as a collector would be great but not outstanding.

What gives him his particular position arises first from his interest and enthusiasm for the new Italian scholarship and for the editions of many hitherto unknown great works of antiquity; secondly, his continuous patronage of scholars and writers; and thirdly, his munificent gifts to the University of Oxford.

His contact with Italian writers was primarily the work of Zano Castiglione, bishop of Bayeux, who visited England about 1432: presumably this was when he met Gloucester. The two men certainly had much in common in their love of books, and when in 1434 Zano attended the Council of Basel as the representative of Henry VI, he devoted some of his time to inquiring for books wanted by Gloucester—especially works by Guarino and Bruni. When the Council adjourned to Florence, Zano found himself in a great centre of scholars and scribes, and made known to many the duke's interests and generosity. From this time onwards, there was a flow of volumes from Italian scholars, all eager to supply his demands.

We are fortunate enough to have part of the correspondence of one of these—Pier Candido Decembrio—with Humphrey, which reveals what labours went to the formation of a great library at this time. The correspondence opens with a letter sent by Candido through a friend to the duke offering to translate Plato's *Republic* for one whom he knew to be so distinguished. This got no answer, so Candido asked his friend to write again. After a long interval Humphrey replied, warmly welcoming the suggestion. In due course Book v of the *Republic* was completed and forwarded to the duke, who was displeased to find that there was no dedicatory epistle to him.

Candido was asked to speed up the translation of the whole work and also to send the promised dedication, when he would find the duke to be a generous friend. Candido's reply is illuminating. He explains that the whole work will be dedicated to Humphrey, but that the individual books were dedicated to a number of friends—presumably with the hope of a reward. The five books already translated were to be written out in a worthy style, and they eventually reached Humphrey, together with a long dedicatory epistle, lauding the duke as a patron of learning and declaring that his name was a by-word among Italian humanists. This beautifully written volume, with its many handsome initials, is now in the British Museum, and on the back of its last leaf is written in the duke's handwriting: 'Cest livre est A moy Homfrey duc de Gloucestre du don P. Candidus secretaire du duc de Milan.'

On receiving the book Gloucester sent a lengthy reply, expressing his pleasure in receiving so important and noble a work on statesmanship which, he says, will never leave his side either at home or on military service. He exhorts Candido to complete the other books of the *Republic* which are eagerly awaited, and to let him know of any works of great value that can be obtained. Candido may be sure that the duke will reward him liberally. In due course the whole work was brought to England by a personal friend of the translator, and furthermore Candido was kept busy searching out, or having copies made of books required by Humphrey. The two scholars did not always agree on items to be provided; Gloucester insisting on certain works being obtained, despite their known faults, while Candido was unwilling to provide such tainted wares. Lists of books were constantly passing to and fro, and Candido was responsible for adding many volumes to the collection. For all this no doubt he was well paid, but not as well as he had hoped, for the correspondence ends with a letter from him to Gloucester in which his disappointment is clear. Gloucester's performances as a patron had evidently not lived up to his promises.

A number of other Italian scholars can be mentioned who were in touch with Gloucester—Piero del Monte, Lapo da Castiglionchio, Antonio Pasini of Todi—all of whom helped him in his endeavours to get the books he wanted. Further evidence of his interest in the humanists is found in the scholarly men from abroad whom he had about him as secretaries. Outstanding among these were Antonio di Beccaria and Titus Livius of Ferrara. The former made translations of a number of treatises of St Athanasius, and more interesting, as showing something of the duke's personal tastes, he also translated into Latin the *Corbaccio* of Boccaccio, in a preface to which Antonio comments on his patron's knowledge of the writings of Boccaccio. Titus Livius, 'poet and orator', himself tells us that poverty drove him to England, where he sought the patronage of the duke in whose household he lived for some time. Humphrey set him to work, writing the life of Henry V, and helped him by contributing much personal information. Titus Livius was also greatly interested in medicine and science, and this made him of added value to his master.

In one way and another therefore, Gloucester was in close touch with Italian scholars and the exciting work which they were doing in making the New Learning available. Before he died his library contained much that had hitherto been unknown in any English collection, or known only in a debased or incomplete form. As the century wore on English scholars were to make the journey to Italy to learn at the fountain source, or to bring back many treasures, but it is to Humphrey, duke of Gloucester, that the pioneer's laurels must go.

To turn nearer home, while still a young man, Humphrey was looked on as a great patron by English poets, and his interest in the works of antiquity must not allow us to forget the part he played in the production of our own literature. As will be seen later (p. 86) Hoccleve translated into verse one of the stories from the *Gesta Romanorum* solely in hope of pleasing Humphrey, and John Lydgate wrote an epithalamium at the time of his marriage to Jacqueline. Later he undertook a verse translation of Laurent de Premierfait's prose version of Boccaccio's *De Casibus Virorum Illustrium*, in which diverse celebrated persons from the time of Adam relate their fortunes and misfortunes. Dealt with in Lydgate's prolix style, this work, which was commissioned by the duke, ran to some 36,000 lines, and intercalated in the narrative are some verses by Lydgate which illustrate the attitude of writers towards a patron. The first set was written 'at the time of translating Boccaccio's book', when, knowing Gloucester's tastes, Lydgate uses medical, nautical and financial metaphors freely. In involved and recondite language he emphasizes his debility through lack of funds, constantly telling Gloucester that 'gold is a cordial', or that the readiest way to renew his energies is by a gift of plate or of money. For eight stanzas Lydgate harps on his theme, and concludes with the hope that a satisfying medicine (of gold, understood) will be forthcoming.

By a lucky chance, later in the poem we have a set of verses which show that Humphrey has played up. Lydgate likens himself to a tired, thirsty pilgrim, appalled at the poetic journey still to be accomplished, his purse empty, his wits dulled by poverty, so that he nearly abandoned his task, but then Humphrey restored him and brought gladness to his heart. The mists of despair and dread cleared away, so he tells us, and Trust, Faith and Hope took their place—and the remaining 25,000 lines of the poem were safely concluded!

It has been worth while to follow Lydgate, despite his verbiage, since he enables us to see Humphrey, like other rich men of his time, as the patron whose aid is essential if the writer is to exist. It cannot be doubted that the knowledge that so ardent a collector was in their midst was an immense encouragement to English writers, as works by Capgrave, Upton and other men survive to show. Nor was the duke content to accept works without comment. From one author we learn that the duke's advice taught him how to write metrically, and how Gloucester would mark with his pencil passages requiring emendation.

Humphrey's renown as a collector of books not only attracted writers and translators to look to him as their patron, but encouraged the University of Oxford to appeal to him to alleviate their bookish poverty. He had previously helped them in a modest way, but in November 1439, in response to a further appeal, he sent them 120 volumes, and later in February 1444 another 135 volumes. These, and other gifts, must have amounted to some 300 manuscripts—a princely donation to a University which at this time was almost without books. In acknowledging the gift of 120 volumes the University stated that they were worth £1000, while several letters tell of their usefulness, and of how they were eagerly consulted by men coming from all parts of the kingdom. The duke's benefactions comprised many standard works in theology philosophy, history, medicine and astrology, as well as a number of works by classical authors and by the Italian poets. 'We wish you could see the students bending over your books in their greediness and thirst for knowledge', the University writes to the duke, and before long the problem of accommodation for the books and readers became acute; and his library and the other books of the University found a home in the new Divinity School, where to this day in 'Duke Humphrey's End' scholars work in the very chamber that first housed this great benefaction.

By 1444, however, Gloucester's days were numbered, and although he promised to give to the University the rest of his Latin books, together with £100 towards the building of the Divinity School, death overtook him before he could carry this out. His last years saw him but the shadow of his former self. The young king was alienated from him. The queen and her supporters did all they could to minimize his power and to throw scorn on his council. At the last he was removed from the Privy Council and denied access to the king, and finally it was resolved to summon Parliament, 'the which Parliament was maad only for to sle the noble Duke', writes the chronicler.

Gloucester must have known something of the

dangers which beset him as he started out to obey the summons to attend Parliament on a cold winter's day in February 1447. Half a mile outside Bury St Edmunds, where Parliament was sitting, he was met by two servants of the royal household, who told him that since the weather was so 'cold and biting' the king excused him from presenting himself at court and desired him to ride straight to his lodgings on the north side of the town. It was about eleven o'clock in the morning when he came into Bury through the South Gate, passed through the horse market, and turning to his left, rode along a mean and squalid street. He called to a passer-by, asking him the name of the street. 'Forsoothe, my Lord, hit is called the Dede Lane', was the reply. 'And then the good Duke remembered him of an olde prophesye that he hadde radde mony a daye before, and seyde, "As our Lord wylle, be hit all".' He continued on his way, and left the town by the North Gate, and soon came to his lodging in St Saviour's Hospital—'the North Spytall called Seynt Salvatoures'.

Soon after this his dinner was served, and then he was called on by five great nobles of the realm, one of whom, Viscount Beaumont, High Constable of England, told him that by the king's command he was under arrest. His own attendants were removed, and a serjeant with two yeomen of the guard took charge of the duke's person. This was on Saturday. During the following week, cut off from his friends and retainers, he slowly lapsed into a state of coma, from which he recovered sufficiently to make his last confession and to receive the sacrament, before he sank again and died about three in the afternoon of Thursday, 23 February 1447.

Was he murdered, or was his end the natural end of a man of over fifty, worn out by debauchery, disappointment and disgrace? Contemporary opinion does not help, since every possible view is voiced, so that we are thrown back on surmise. That the duke was in disgrace is clear. His enemies were in the ascendant, and the removal of Gloucester was certainly to their convenience, since he was the obvious and most influential person who could have opposed the policies of the ambitious and energetic queen, Margaret of Anjou, and her chief agent, the duke of Suffolk. The duke's departure from the political scene undoubtedly made things easier for the queen's party. Part of his great wealth and possessions came their way, and the execution and disgrace of his immediate followers was a warning to others who opposed the régime. If Suffolk and his friends wanted to get rid of Humphrey it would not have been difficult for them to have administered a slow poison during the five days he was *incommunicado* in St Saviour's Hospital.

Efforts were made to convince everyone that he had come to no violent end, and on the day after his death his body was publicly exposed, and 'whosoever wolde come, saugh hym dede'. In fact, all this did was to show that he was not mutilated in any way, but it did no more. However, on the following day, just a week after his arrival at Bury, his corpse started on his last journey to St Albans, escorted by twenty torches only, and unaccompanied by those whom his rank would have made seemly. By slow stages the cortège reached the abbey which he loved so well, and there, surrounded by his faithful servants only, he was laid in a 'fair vault', and so came to an end the life of the 'good Duke', son and brother of kings, who for forty years had played a prominent part in the great affairs of the realm. The story of his life and death is yet another of those examples of the turn of Fortune's wheel, so that one who

> stood in greet prosperitee
> Is yffalen out of heigh degree
> Into myserie, and endeth wrecchedly.

SIR JOHN FASTOLF

By a malign stroke of fortune one of the most famous of English captains in the French wars of the first half of the fifteenth century was transformed by Shakespeare's pen from Fastolf to Falstaff, and as such came to be known as one of his greatest comic characters—a liar, a braggart, a 'bag of guts', a wit, a friend of rogues and ne'er-do-wells; in short—everything which Fastolf was not. How this change or confusion came about need not concern us here: our interest is to follow the fortunes of a well-to-do professional soldier of the fifteenth century, who in the course of a long life acquired great riches and reputation.

The Fastolfs were a well-known Norfolk family of many branches, one of which settled at Caister, near Yarmouth, and there John Fastolf was born about 1378. His father had inherited Caister and other manors, and had also bought much property in Norfolk, so that the young Fastolf spent the earliest years of his life in comfortable surroundings, and then probably found himself, as was the custom of the day, at some seven or eight years of age sent to live in the household of a friend or acquaintance, where as a page he would be called upon to perform minor services for his lord and lady. As he waited on them in hall and in bower many important and many trivial details of everyday life and manners would be borne in on him. With good fortune he would learn to read, and even to write; to speak correctly; to play upon some instrument; to dance; to perform simple services with horse and hound.

At the age of twelve or thirteen more serious things would begin to occupy the boy's time. Instead of spending many hours in the lady's bower he would be mainly engaged in his lord's affairs, such as the 'manage' of the horse, the complicated ritual of the hunt, the care of hounds and of hawks and how to look after his master's armour and weapons. When his lord rode out he would attend him and would await anxiously while the outcome of the battle or the tourney was uncertain. At home he would greet the guests on their arrival, showing them to their quarters, waiting on their needs and proving himself to be a young man of quality as he ministered to them. By the cultivation of his abilities in these ways he hoped to deserve his title of esquire, and could look forward to further chances of showing valour and gentleness in war and peace and to advancement in his career.

Some such training as this was in all probability the lot of John Fastolf, since in his early twenties he was sufficiently well-trained and spoken of to be included in the retinue of Henry IV's second son, Thomas of Lancaster, who was sent to Ireland as the king's deputy in 1401. Ireland at this time was in an unsettled condition and the king's forces were often hard put to it to keep a semblance of control. Thus, soon after his arrival, Thomas of Lancaster found himself without funds and shut up in a small town in Kildare, protected by a small force, of whom Fastolf was one. This early taste of the ardours of soldiering taught Fastolf what to expect during the next few years in Ireland where he lived until 1410 or 1411. His lord, it is true, was in England from time to time, and Fastolf may have been with him, but it was in the routine of policing an occupied area, ever likely to burst into revolt, that Fastolf obtained much experience of the day-to-day soldier's life that he was to live for some forty years.

While in Ireland his mother, two years before her death in 1406, had given him Caister and a neighbouring manor of Repps, and he increased his resources by his marriage in January 1409 with Milicent, widow of Sir Stephen Scrope, the right-hand man of Thomas of Lancaster. Fastolf must have stood well in the eyes of men to have looked thus high with success, and on his marriage he became master of the fine estate of Castle Combe in Wiltshire as well as of other manors in Yorkshire. He was by now sufficiently well off to settle £100 a year on his wife for her own use—a not inconsiderable sum at a time when the local curate served for £10 a year, and an income of £5 a year was reckoned by Sir John Fortescue to be 'a fair living for a yeoman'.

Thomas of Lancaster left Ireland for the last time in the spring of 1409, and we next see Fastolf associated with him in the summer of 1412. For at least a year previous to this Henry IV had been watching the situation in France, hoping to take advantage of the quarrel for supremacy between the houses of Orleans and of Burgundy. In July 1411 the duke of Burgundy had made overtures to Henry, offering his daughter in marriage to the prince of Wales together with other advantages in return for an alliance. The king considered these proposals favourably, but for various reasons postponed an expedition to France in the autumn of 1411. Early in 1412, while negotiations for the marriage were still in progress, a rival party, headed by the dukes of Berry, Bourbon, Orleans and others, sent messages to Henry with large offers, including the restoration of the ancient duchy of Aquitaine, if he would aid them to destroy the power of Burgundy and thus make them supreme in France, since the enfeebled and half-mad king Charles VI was but a pawn in the hands of these mighty opposites. Henry finally agreed to help the dukes, and orders were given for the English forces to muster at Southampton on 23 June, ready to cross to France.

Sickness made it impossible for the king to lead his forces in person; the prince of Wales was out of favour, so the command fell on Thomas of Lancaster who, in July 1412, was created earl of Albemarle and duke of Clarence. In August the duke's forces put out from Southampton, and landed at St Vaast on the Normandy coast. They ravaged the Côtentin, Normandy and Maine, sweeping on through Anjou into the valleys of the Loire and the Indre, meeting with little opposition, for in the words of the Chronicle, 'they ryden forth throughout France, and took castle and town, and slew many Frenchmen that withstood them, and took many prisoners as they rode'.

Much had happened in French politics during that summer, however, for Burgundy had become reconciled with the king, and they had made common cause against the revolting dukes, who were driven from stronghold to stronghold until, after being besieged in Bourges for some time, they came to terms with their opponents and all question of fulfilling their promises to Henry was a thing of the past. As the English forces drew nearer it became urgent to deal with them in some way, and with poetic justice it was agreed that those who brought them in should bribe them to depart. This suited Clarence and his captains well, and they put forward stupendous claims which the luckless dukes met as best they could. Fastolf saw his master advance a claim for 120,000 crowns, and he actually received 40,000 in cash. In addition he was given a crucifix and two crosses, each of them of superlative workmanship, studded with jewels, while the larger of them was enriched with a chip of the Cross and a nail taken from the same. Fastolf occupied too lowly a position in Clarence's retinue for much, if any, of this spoil to have come his way, but he may well have reflected on the glittering opportunities which a successful raid or capture might afford once he was senior enough to claim a share in a successful army's booty.

He may also have noted the ease with which the expedition had obtained such success. The force was a comparatively small one: so far as we can trust medieval figures it appears to have comprised 1500 men-at-arms and 5000 archers, horse-keepers, varlets, etc. Even so, they had conducted what was little worse than a promenade from the coast right across France to Bourges where they were paid off. It was Fastolf's first experience of what was to become so familiar to him for the next thirty years. As the invaders rode through the countryside, the peasantry could offer no opposition, hoping at best that the English would pass by without requisitioning their stock or their transport, and without incidents occurring which might lead to sterner measures. Only when a castle or fortified town stood in the line of march were the English captains forced to deliberate, and ask themselves whether the inhabitants would surrender, and if not, was it safe to proceed leaving a hostile force in their rear, or must the place be besieged and overcome? Unless the place were large and a vital link in communications it could be passed by, or perhaps a small force be detached to besiege it. The main body moved on, scarcely to be arrested until an equal or superior force barred its way. In this first expedition in France Fastolf did not have such an experience, for the English left Bourges after some of the ransom had been paid, and taking hostages with them for the rest, struck south-west for the English province of Guienne, and in due course came into winter quarters at Bordeaux. Here, we are told, they revelled in the warm climate, sallying out from time to time into the neighbouring countryside to replenish their larder.

Although he was still only a squire, Fastolf was rising in importance, for he was made captain of the castle of Veires (Gascony), and when Clarence was recalled to England on the death of Henry IV in March 1413, he made Fastolf deputy constable of Bordeaux. In addition, he was part of the force taken by the new lieutenant of Aquitaine (the earl of Dorset) on a marauding foray in the country north of Bordeaux. Various places were taken, and, in a vigorous attempt by the French to expell the invaders, Fastolf took prisoner one of their leaders—the lord of Soubise. Part of his ransom he not unnaturally paid in the produce of his estate, so that in 1415 Fastolf was licensed to import into England, free of duty, 130 tuns of Gascony wine. In other ways he had less reason to remember with pleasure these days spent in the south, for so late as 1455 he was still petitioning the Crown to pay him £227. 15*s*. 3½*d*. which he alleged was owing to him 'for divers charges and costs by him borne for the time that he occupied the office of the Constabulary of Bordeaux'; while at the same time he asserted that he was owed over £200 'for wages for his service done to the King and to the Duke of Clarence, being the King's Lieutenant in Guienne'. How long a period this covered is uncertain; all we know is that early in 1415 he was back in England.

By then it was commonly understood that preparations were being made for the invasion of France. Everywhere men saw signs of warlike activity. Orders were given to impress ships, and to bring them to Southampton. In the country around the port, herds of beasts were assembled; carpenters, stone-cutters, farriers, brick-makers, smiths and the like were enlisted; carts, timber, guns, engines of war were collected to await the order for embarkation. In addition, the recruitment of the army went on apace. The day was long past when feudal lords could call on their vassals for military service, and in any case, such service was generally for a limited period of forty days, and so would have been useless for overseas purposes. In its place a system had been evolved whereby soldiers entered into a voluntary contract to serve for a specified sum per day, and generally for not less than one hundred days. Their leaders, for their part, executed a formal indenture with the king, or one of the greater nobles, to provide a specified number of men to serve upon closely defined terms, both as to pay and rewards. The squires or men-at-arms received one shilling and the archers sixpence a day, and their payment began as soon as they reported at the assigned mustering place. The king bound himself to pay their wages at specified times, and to find transport for men and their horses; in return, he was entitled to the ransoms of all captives of the highest rank, and to one-third of the ransoms of less exalted men. All spoils of war were to be strictly accounted for, while robbery, pillaging and sacrilege were sternly forbidden. The soldier in France, therefore, was certain not only of his daily pay, but of the chance of rich booty in the form of captives and spoils, should fortune come his way.

To a professional soldier such as Fastolf, the opening up of the war in France again meant much, and on 18 June 1415 he agreed to provide ten men-at-arms and thirty archers to serve for a year in the king's wars, to be paid at the accustomed rates. They were all to come provided with a horse, while the men-at-arms had to produce four horses each, and usually this meant in addition the attendance of at least one horseman, or 'varlet', or groom, to attend to the spare horses. Midsummer Day had been appointed originally for the great muster at Southampton, but if Fastolf and his men were there on time they experienced that well-known army phenomenon—'operational delay'—for they had to hang about all through July, during which time the countryside surrounding Southampton saw more and more men arriving, until the greatest force ever mustered by an English king was ready to embark. Finally, all was complete: on Wednesday 7 August the king embarked in the *Trinity Royal*, and after further delays, four days later the expedition set sail.

Fastolf knew probably no more than others what was to be their landing place, but in the early dawn of Tuesday, 13 August, landfall was made, and later the brick walls of Harfleur with its gates and many towers were clear in the afternoon sun. Early the next morning an unmolested landing was made at Ste Adresse, now a suburb of Havre, and Fastolf may well have taken up his lodging near the priory at Granville, a mile or so to the west of Harfleur, where his old master, the duke of Clarence, had his quarters. A few days passed in the necessary business of getting everything on shore, and in reconnoitring the situation before the siege was begun. Since the next twenty years and more of Fastolf's life were to be spent in besieging towns and castles some description of such operations is, perhaps, appropriate.

Once a town was closely invested, and all means of getting in or out sealed off, the first problem to settle was how to bring about its surrender most quickly. There was always hope of treachery within, or of a surrender on terms. Given time, the garrison could be starved out; given suitable conditions their water supply could be cut off or poisoned; given favourable terrain the walls could be breached or scaled without overwhelming losses. On the other hand, enemy forces from elsewhere might arrive in such numbers as to cause the attackers to retreat, or the defences might be too strong, and the garrison too powerful to be overcome. Here is a detailed account of the siege of Carlisle (1315), written by an inhabitant, which may serve as an example of what such things were like, as conditions changed very little in the succeeding century:

> Soon afterwards in that same year, on the feast of St Mary Magdalene [22 July], the king of Scotland assembled all his forces and came to Carlisle, where he compassed the city round about and besieged it for ten days, treading all the crops under foot, ravaging the suburbs with the surrounding country, and burning throughout all those parts; moreover he drove a vast spoil of cattle to feed his army, from Allerdale and Coupland and Westmorland. So on each day of the siege they

made an assault against one of the three city gates, and sometimes at all three together, yet never with impunity. For we cast upon them from the wall javelins and arrows and stones, both then and at other times, in such multitude and number that they enquired one of the other, 'Do stones increase and multiply, then, within these walls?' Moreover on the fifth day of the siege they set up an engine for casting stones hard by Trinity Church, where the king had pitched his tent; and they threw great stones without intermission against the wall and the Calden gate; yet with all this they did little or no harm to the townsfolk, save only that they slew one man. For we had seven or eight such engines in the city, without reckoning other engines of war, namely, the so-called springalds, for hurling long javelins, which wrought much terror and havoc among the besiegers. So in the meanwhile the Scots set up a great Belfry, like a tower, which far overtopped the town walls; whereupon the city carpenters, upon one tower against which this belfry must have been set if it had been brought up to the wall, built another tower of wood that overtopped that belfry. But the Scottish engine never came against the wall; for when men dragged it on its wheels over the wet and miry ground, there it stuck fast with its own weight, nor could they draw it forward or harm us. Moreover the Scots had made long ladders, which they had brought with them for scaling the wall in divers places, and a sow[1] for undermining the town wall if possible; but neither ladders nor sow availed them. Again, they made a multitude of fascines of corn and hay to fill the water-moat without the wall towards the east, that they might thus cross it dry-shod; and long wooden bridges that ran on wheels, which they hoped to draw so strongly and swiftly with ropes as to pass that broad moat. Yet, for all the time of this siege, neither could the fascines fill the ditch nor those bridges pass it; but their weight dragged them to the bottom. So on the ninth day, when all their engines were ready, they made a general assault on all the city gates and

[1] *sow*: a movable structure having a strong roof, used to cover men advancing to the walls of a besieged place and to protect them while engaged in sapping and mining operations.

around the whole wall; manfully they came on, and our townsfolk also defended themselves like men; and likewise again on the morrow. Now the Scots here used that same wile whereby they had taken the castle of Edinburgh; for they caused the greater part of their host to make an assault upon the eastern part of the city, against the Franciscan Friary, that they might draw the defenders thither. Meanwhile the lord James Douglas, a bold and crafty knight, with others of the doughtiest and most active of that army, arrayed themselves on the west against the convents of the Canons and of the Friars Preachers, where the defences were so high and difficult of access that no assault was expected. There they reared long ladders whereby they climbed up; and they had a great host of archers who shot thick and close, that no man might show his head over the wall. Yet, blessed be God! they found such a welcome there that they and their ladders were flung to the earth; at which place and elsewhere around the wall some were slain and some taken and some wounded. So on the eleventh day, to wit on the feast of St Peter *ad vincula*, either because they had tidings of an English host coming to raise the siege, or because they despaired of further success, the Scots retired in confusion at daybreak to their own land, leaving behind all their engines of war aforesaid.

At Harfleur the English decided to take the place by bringing the whole of their forces into action as quickly and vigorously as possible. To this end Clarence was ordered to work his way round to the east side of the town so as to prevent any relieving force approaching from that side. He was successful in this, and by the morning of 19 August had occupied the hills on the north-east of Harfleur, and the wretched inhabitants saw that he had with him a number of cannon with which to bombard their walls. Meanwhile, the king was busily at work on other sides of the town, and a continuous heavy onslaught with stones flung by various siege engines began to weaken the walls. At the same time squads of miners were at work. Protected by wooden screens, which they pushed before them, the tunnellers drove their mines towards the walls, hoping to burrow beneath them, or at least to undermine them so that they would collapse. They did much damage by these means, but no sooner had a breach been made than it was filled in as soon as darkness fell. Little by little the attackers approached the walls, only to be met by a devastating fusillade of stones, arrows, scalding liquids, chalk, quick-lime, etc., which frustrated their attempts to scale the walls by ladder or tower and prevented them from breaking down the walls themselves.

To overcome these difficulties screens were made of great piles of faggots behind which a trench was dug up to the wall of the town so that it could be undermined. In other ways the main forces were unceasing in their attack: the 'King's Daughter' and her 'Maidens', as the siege guns were called were hard at work, while the king and his lieutenants were everywhere employing every device they knew to bring about an early capitulation. After three weeks of this the French were in sore plight: no help was forthcoming from the French forces outside Harfleur; food was running out; the walls were breached and many houses had been destroyed. No wonder that on the morning of 18 September just before sun-up the garrison sent a message to Clarence, offering to surrender the town if no help reached them within four days.

None came; and on the 22nd the English host witnessed the capitulation. Five hundred English soldiers appeared at the gates of Harfleur and demanded the surrender of the town. In due time, forth came the captain of the garrison with others, wearing the shirts of penitence, ropes round their necks and bearing the keys. When they came to Henry's regally adorned pavilion, at first he would not see them, but having kept them kneeling for a time, at last he received them, and spared their lives. He appointed the earl of Dorset as captain of the town, and later in the autumn Fastolf was named as his lieutenant.

In the five weeks that had passed since the landing Fastolf had good reason to realize that the hazards of war were not confined to the incidents of battle and siege, for he saw men struck down on all sides with fevers and dysentery, or the flux as it was then called. The conditions around Harfleur favoured these diseases. The many surrounding swamps, the rotting carcasses, the offal of the slaughtered animals, the infected air did their deadly work. Men were in no condition to resist, since they were short of rations, and naturally ate avidly of the fruits and shell-fish of the Normandy orchards and creeks. It is said that some 2000 died in the course of the siege, while Fastolf saw his old chief, the duke of Clarence, and hundreds of others stricken with sickness, carried down to the ships and taken back to England.

Fastolf himself was unharmed and soon was on 'the most foolhardy and reckless adventure that ever an unreasoning pietist devised', as he followed Henry out of Harfleur on the proceedings which led to the field of Agincourt on 25 October 1415. The story of that day needs no retelling, and (alas!) John Fastolf's own story remains for ever unknown. Like others who outlived that day and came safe home he may have feasted his friends and told of his exploits—but for the time being, home was not for him, and before long he was back in Harfleur where the earl of Dorset was struggling to repair the damage and to put the town into a condition to withstand any French attack.

Not content with a passive role, the duke probed the countryside for miles around, bringing back welcome supplies and information as to the enemy. Late in November he gave Fastolf charge of a considerable force which swept up the valley of the Seine to within a few miles of Rouen. It was a gambler's throw: at one moment Fastolf had 500 prisoners, but later in the raid they were attacked, and returned without prisoners and with their own ranks depleted. A few weeks later a more successful raid was made, and early in the new year a fresh force arrived, and the old garrison was withdrawn.

Not Fastolf, however. He was promoted and henceforth ranks as one of the three lieutenants of the earl of Dorset. As soon as better weather came, the English forces began another series of forays. In one of the most spectacular of these Fastolf was involved. Starting from Harfleur on the evening of 9 March 1416, the earl and a force of some thousand men set out on a three-day raid. All went well at first: they burnt and ravaged at will, but then found that a superior force had moved in behind them, and cut them off from their base. In the fight that followed the English were defeated, but managed to withdraw their broken forces under cover of night, and by abandoning their baggage-train and horses got nearly back to Harfleur before the enemy overtook them. Exhausted though they were, the English fought with the courage of desperation on the marshes a few miles from Harfleur, and at the last moment snatched victory from their opponents, took many hundreds of them prisoner, and so marched in triumph home again.

It was but a Pyrrhic victory, and during the coming months as he surveyed the decimated forces under his command, and watched the French investing the town ever more closely, both by land and by sea, Fastolf must have regretted the men thrown away in a series of futile raids. For the situation within Harfleur was grim as summer wore on. Only one ship had successfully run the blockade: people were dying of starvation and the price of such foodstuffs as were available was tremendous. Week after week went by, with hope failing, but at last in August a large English fleet appeared, and after a seven-hour battle won the day, and brought relief to the hard-pressed garrison. It was just over a year since Fastolf had landed at Ste Adresse.

We cannot follow Fastolf in this detailed fashion throughout his military career, and, after all, the soldier's life at all times is something lacking in variety, but much may still usefully be said in illustration of a typical soldier-of-fortune's career in the fifteenth century. After his stay in Harfleur he returned to England, but in 1417 found himself with many others at the familiar business of making indentures, mustering troops and reporting for service overseas. The delays this time were more than usually prolonged and the army did not sail until the end of July, and did not make for Harfleur as was expected, but after two days came to shore at Touques (Trouville). The duke of Clarence, now recovered from his sickness, was made constable of the army; it is almost certain that Fastolf was under his immediate command, and it was about this time that he was knighted.

Within a fortnight Clarence moved off to invest Caen, and on 14 August took up his quarters at the famous Abbaye des Dames, a strongly fortified place on the eastern side of the town. Fortune favoured him and he took the Abbaye des Hommes on the west by surprise, and when Henry arrived on 18 August the town was surrounded and violent siege operations began—battery, mining, cannonade all helping to damage the defences and to weaken the opposition. On 4 September Clarence got a foothold, and to the cries of 'A Clarence, a Clarence, a Saint George', first the streets and then the castle were taken amidst scenes of fierce hand-to-hand combats and furious resistance.

No sooner was Caen reduced than Fastolf was off again, and was at the taking of the castle at Courcy on 1 October, at Seéz a few days later, and before the end of the month saw the stronghold of Alençon surrender without striking a blow. After this he was soon encamped outside the great fortress of Falaise. Here in the cold December days of 1417, Fastolf and others got what comfort they could by sheltering in extemporized huts which they set up on the frozen plain. They were protected from attack by a trench and palisade and lay between the enemy and any possible relief, waiting for shortage of food to do much to weaken the besieged. A continuous cannonade was maintained and after three weeks the town surrendered. As was so often the case the castle within was still strongly fortified and protected, and some very strenuous attacks and fierce fighting were necessary before the garrison surrendered on 16 February.

Fastolf had small time to rest, as he soon left the town in the wake of Clarence who had orders to clear and consolidate the eastern fringes of the occupied territory. Many places capitulated without a struggle or at best with only a token one. As an exception, at Harcourt, a fifteen days' siege was necessary, but it was worth it, since a great treasure of money and jewels was part of the booty. Another hardly-won place was the Benedictine Abbey of Bec-Hellouin, which was taken from the monks by the French, and used by them as a fortified strong point against the duke, who lost three weeks in subduing them before he could pass on in safety.

It was now early June, and the command was taken over by the king himself, who spent three weeks in the siege of Louviers, and four weeks in reducing Pont de l'Arche (thus obtaining control of the famous bridge over the Seine) before he was able to move into the attack on the glittering prize of Rouen. Viewed on a summer's morning in the last days of July 1418 it must have presented a magnificent sight to Fastolf's eyes. The city lay on the right bank of the Seine and was enclosed by a wall, five miles in circumference, reinforced by a deep ditch, and having some sixty towers each armed with guns. The five great gates were heavily protected with flanking towers and outworks, and the whole presented a formidable problem to an enemy's eye. Within the walls, rising high above a jumble of roofs, was the magnificent cathedral with its one superb tower at the western end (the Tour de Beurre was not commenced until 1485), while the great height of the nave dwarfed all within its range. On all sides could be seen churches, abbeys, palaces and rich merchants' houses which made even the buildings of the city of London seem insignificant.

Within the walls thousands from the surrounding

countryside had hurried as the English troops drew near, and these extra mouths formed an additional embarrassment to the defenders when it was seen that Henry proposed to starve them into submission. A tight cordon was thrown round the city, and the whole perimeter was divided into four sections—that on the west under the command of the duke of Clarence. The besieged were far from quiet. They flung missiles of various sorts into the English camps, and from time to time surged out from one of the gates in a surprise attack. All in vain. The English forces drove them back, and within a couple of months food and water began to run out. Nothing could slacken the hold the besiegers had on the city, and Fastolf and the other captains had little more to do but to see that the business of 'holding the line' was faithfully discharged. This meant the keeping of the deep trenches which ran from one strong-point to another in repair; maintaining a twenty-four hour watch on all enemy movements; dealing with deserters and break-outs which were attempted from time to time. As conditions within the city worsened, numbers of women and children, the old and the maimed, were thrust out into no-man's-land, to live or die as best they could. The English fed them, but kept them penned in between the two armies, until after much suffering the defenders asked for terms. These were agreed to after considerable haggling, and on 20 January 1419 Henry and his captains rode in triumph into the city to give thanks at the great cathedral.

Sir John was not given much leisure to see for himself the many wonders of Rouen, for in a few days he was off with Clarence to subdue 'the residue of Normandy'. Castle after castle yielded to the English and on 3 February

Fastolf found himself captain of Fécamp, which had surrendered two days earlier. We know nothing of his movements for the rest of the year, but he was probably in the train of Clarence as he steadily worked his way up the river in the summer of 1419, even making a brief armed demonstration before the gates of Paris itself.

All through the coming autumn and winter Fastolf and his like were kept busy with the innumerable tasks incident to holding down a conquered country, and they only heard through gossip how negotiations with the various French and Burgundian parties kept the fortunes of Henry in continual suspense, until the treaty of Troyes and his marriage to the king's daughter, Catherine, in June 1420, seemed to have brought to Henry the fruition of his desires—the ultimate union of the two crowns.

Not all Frenchmen were so easily satisfied, and soon steps had to be taken to subdue the forces who opposed the treaty, and within a fortnight of Henry's marriage Fastolf found himself part of a large force besieging Montereau, and after that Melun. The latter proved a hard nut to crack and took from 13 July until 17 November to subdue. From there Fastolf was moved down the Seine to Paris, and made captain of the Bastille, one of the English garrisons within the city, for Henry was not loved in the capital, and sufficient forces had to be maintained, in case of trouble.

The next year, 1421, opened badly, for Fastolf's old chief, Clarence, was killed at the battle of Baugé (Maine-et-Loire). Whether Fastolf was with him or not, we do not know. He had been given a licence to buy grain for the Bastille as recently as February, and so may have been in Paris when the news of the battle reached the city on

Friday 4 April. As we have seen, he had been attached to the duke ever since 1401, and with the passing of Clarence the first phase of his life as a soldier ends.

The second phase of Fastolf's military service was also one of twenty years, during which his reputation and responsibilities steadily increased. Instead of the duke of Clarence, another of the king's brothers, the duke of Bedford, became his master: a steady, disciplined soldier and statesman, in place of an impetuous improviser. Fastolf was made his Master of Household in January 1422, a post of considerable responsibility; and, since at that time and for long after Bedford was constantly engrossed in affairs of State, Fastolf must have been in supreme command, and no doubt it was his general ability that saw him appointed the king's lieutenant in Normandy, and governor of Anjou and Maine in 1423.

His policy was one of action. At Pacy (Eure) he captured Guillaume Raymond, governor of the city, who agreed to pay him 3200 salutes in gold for a ransom, but to Fastolf's chagrin, Raymond was claimed by his superior, Bedford, and carried off by him. An even more glittering prize came his way the next summer, for at the battle of Verneuil, in August 1424, Fastolf and Lord Willoughby took the duke of Alençon prisoner, and agreed with him on the sum of 40,000 marks as a fitting ransom. In due course this was paid, but Fastolf to the end of his life protested that he had never been given his share of the ransom-money. Earlier in the year he had agreed with Bedford to find eighty men-at-arms and 240 archers to take part in the campaign in Maine—an indication of his present importance when we remember that he provided only ten and thirty when he went to France in 1415, or that at the same time even the duke of York accounted for no more than 100 and 300. Furthermore, he was raised to the dignity of a knight banneret in 1423, having been knighted (as we have seen) sometime before January 1418.

The year 1425 was a memorable one for him. His energetic campaigning saw Maine subjected, in the course of which many strongholds were taken. In particular he could recall with pride the surrender of Mons, of St Ouen D'Estrais, of Beaumont le Vicomte, and lastly of the castle of Silly-Guillem. It was from this last place that he took the title of Baron of Silly-Guillem in France, and his achievements were recognized in England by his election as a Knight of the Garter—an honour the more to be esteemed since it came to him only after the duke of Bedford had weighed his merits against those of Sir John Ratcliffe, and had pronounced in his favour.

So the years went on. We find him at times in England, for the annual Garter ceremonies, or on his own affairs, but most of the time he is to be found with a good force at his back following Bedford in the varied fortunes of the struggle with France. He had many responsibilities, although to his great annoyance he was superseded as Governor of Maine and Anjou by John, Lord Talbot, in 1426, and henceforth had to be content with captaincies of centres such as Caen. Furthermore, as the war went against the English, he had the misery of seeing much that he had helped to win taken away.

Before this, however, there were two engagements in which he was a participator, one of which marked the height of his military career; the other, his temporary eclipse. The first took place in February 1429, when

Fastolf was in charge of a force sent to protect a food convoy coming from Paris to bring supplies to the English army outside Orleans. The French got wind of this, and forces were sent to intercept them. The convoy presented an easy target as the four hundred wagons laden with grain and fish lumbered along towards the village of Rouvrai-Saint-Denis, apparently fearing no attack, and with little order or discipline. Fortunately for them, the French and their Scottish allies had been ordered not to attack until the count of Clermont, their leader, had joined them. This gave Fastolf time to prepare. He grouped his wagons so as to form an enclosure, open at two points only. At one of these he stationed his French mercenaries, behind a palisade of sharpened stakes; at the other, his English bowmen. Impatient at the delay of their leader, and ignoring orders not to dismount, the Scottish men-at-arms left their horses, and rushed on the archers sword in hand, followed by some of their French companions. At the other entrance a cavalry charge found itself impaled and easily slaughtered or put to flight. A swift sortie of the defenders from this side of the enclosure enabled them to fall from behind on the Scottish and French forces on the other side, and in a few minutes all was over. Fastolf and his men proceeded, and brought the much-needed Lenten fare to the besiegers outside Orleans. Thus ended the so-called battle of the Herrings—a notable feather in Fastolf's cap.

Later in the year he was not so fortunate, for not only was he on the losing side, but was also accused of cowardice. The facts were as follows. In June, in response to a request from Lord Talbot, Fastolf was dispatched from Paris with a well-equipped force some 5000 strong to relieve the English besieged in Beaugency on the Loire. When they joined Talbot they found that Beaugency had surrendered, and they were uncertain what to do. The French troops under the influence of Joan of Arc had recently raised the siege of Orleans; and flushed with victory, and powerfully inspired by the Maid, were on the offensive. At the English council of war Fastolf and Talbot were at odds. Fastolf was for retiring, in order to give the troops time to rest, to await reinforcements, and to recover their morale, shaken by the Maid's successes. Talbot's pride would not allow of this, and he declared that if the enemy came, he would fight them. The debate was furious, but was broken off by news that the advance-guard of the enemy, some 1500 mounted men, was rapidly approaching. There was nothing for it but to take up the best position possible. The vanguard, baggage and artillery were drawn up alongside the hedges, while the main body tried to fall back to take up their stand between a wood and the fortified church of Patay. To protect this manœuvre Talbot and his 500 archers were to hold the narrow road along which the French would advance.

At first the French scouts could not make contact, but fortunately for them, they startled a stag who ran among the English troops, who betrayed their position by loud cries and hallos. Before any complete disposition of the English forces could be made, the French horsemen fell on Talbot and overran him. There was a panic: the captain of the vanguard, thinking all was lost, abandoned his position and fled, his men following his white standard.

Amidst all the confusion and noise Fastolf had to act. One who was with him (*moy acteur estant present*) tells us what happened. He writes:

Sir John Fastolf, then perceiving the danger of this flight, and seeing that all was going wrong, was now advised to save himself; but when he was told that he had best look after his own person, since the battle was lost, he was fain at all risks to enter the field again, and there await such fortune as our Lord should please to send him; saying that he would sooner die or be taken prisoner than shamefully to fly and so abandon his people. And while he was even yet hesitating to leave, the French had overpowered Lord Talbot, who was himself taken prisoner and all his men were slain.... Thus, as you hear, went this affair, which when Sir John Fastolf saw, he took his departure much against his will, attended with a very small company, and expressing the deepest sorrow that man ever felt; and, of a truth, he would have gone back to the battle, had it not been for those who were with him, especially John, Bastard of Thian, and others who dissuaded him, and so he took his way to Estampes.

Naturally his action did not go without question, and at first his master took a severe view of what he had done, and deprived him of his Garter. Later on, however, when Bedford had had time to consider the facts, the Garter was restored to him, and he continued to enjoy the favour of the duke. Unfortunately for Fastolf's reputation in subsequent ages, the chronicler Monstrelet gave a very hostile interpretation of Fastolf's conduct, which was accepted by English chroniclers, read by Shakespeare, and given dramatic expression in the *First Part of Henry VI*

> *Falst.* My gracious sovereign, as I rode from Calais,
> To haste unto your coronation,
> A letter was deliver'd to my hands,
> Writ to your Grace from th' Duke of Burgundy.
> *Talbot.* Shame to the Duke of Burgundy and thee!
> I vow'd, base knight, when I did meet thee next,
> To tear the garter from thy craven's leg, [*Plucking it off.*
> Which I have done, because unworthily

Thou wast installed in that high degree.
Pardon me, princely Henry and the rest:
This dastard, at the battle of Patay,
When but in all I was six thousand strong
And that the French were almost ten to one,
Before we met or that a stroke was given,
Like to a trusty squire did run away;
In which assault we lost twelve hundred men;
Myself and divers gentlemen beside
Were there surprised and taken prisoners.
Then judge, great lords, if I have done amiss;
Or whether that such cowards ought to wear
This ornament of knighthood, yea or no.
Glouc. To say the truth, this fact was infamous,
And ill beseeming any common man,
Much more a knight, a captain and a leader.

Here, perhaps, is a fitting moment to leave Fastolf's military career. Ten more years were to pass before he came home for good: years in which he was continuously active, but in which the English hold on France was being steadily weakened. The old soldier's wisdom and competence were recognized on all sides: he was one of the English representatives at the negotiations of the peace of Arras; his views on the future conduct of the war in France were formally requested; on the death of Bedford he was one of the executors of his will. But the great days were over. Much of Normandy, Anjou, Maine and the Île de France he must have known better than his native Norfolk, and could scarcely have remembered the many places he had stormed, or the encounters he had been in since first he landed in France. Some things he did not forget: the unpaid ransoms of his prisoners and the sums owing to him for his services, and his loans. He retired to England about 1440 to settle down to nurse his grievances and to show a very active interest in protecting and increasing his already considerable wealth and property. To this we may now turn.

By a fortunate chance we know a good deal about Fastolf's life after he retired from active service which throws much light on his qualities and disposition. He was friendly with the famous Norfolk family of the Pastons, and among their papers many letters and documents from Fastolf have survived. It is from these in large part that we are enabled to construct his life in England from about 1440 onwards. It will be remembered that he had inherited property in Yarmouth and Norwich, in particular the manors of Caister and Repps just outside Yarmouth, which remained the centre of his possessions all his life, while in addition he added by purchase manors in many East Anglian counties, and also by his marriage in January 1409 became master of the lands of his wife Milicent, widow of Sir Stephen Scrope, who brought him manors in Wiltshire and in Yorkshire. Fastolf was, therefore, a considerable landlord all his life; and, as we shall see, lost no opportunity of increasing his wealth by shrewd investment and hard bargaining.

Throughout his long service in France his affairs in England took second place, though he crossed the Channel from time to time to be present at the annual Garter ceremonies at Windsor about St George's Day, or to execute the royal command to serve on a county commission to raise forces or to make inquiry into wrongdoings. At such times he was able to attend to his own affairs, lending money, buying and selling land or wardships as occasion offered.

On his return he did not go at once to live on his estates but remained in London, for the Privy Council naturally wanted the advice of so experienced a warrior from time to time. A few years earlier in 1435 he had prepared a detailed report on the conduct of the war, and again in 1448 drew up a report which formed the basis of the instructions given by the king to the duke of Somerset 'for the government of France and Normandy'. As we should expect these reports are the work of a realist: adopt the sternest measures, he says; lose no time and energy in sieges; burn and lay waste the countryside, seeking out the richest and most fertile regions; choose 'goode and notable captains, discrete and konnying in the werre'; waste no time making pacts, for they are worthless—and so on.

As soon as he returned to England Fastolf threw all his energy into the administration of his affairs. His officials heard his voice and trembled. One is ordered to send an answer to each item of business entrusted to him without delay. Another is told to 'send me word who dares be so hardy to kick against you in my right. And tell them on my behalf that they shall be quit as far as law and reason demand. And if they will not fear or obey that [decision] then they shall be quit by Blackbeard or Whitebeard—that is to say, by God or the Devil.' He gives orders to 'sue to the uttermost', or to indict all who served on a jury against him whatever the cost. 'Forget not that old shrew Dalling', he writes, 'for he is sore at my stomach.' But perhaps the general nature of Fastolf's day-to-day correspondence may best be seen by quoting a typical letter sent to his agent in Norfolk. It runs:

Right trusty and well beloved friend, I thank you for the quittance of Richard Sellyng you have sent me by William Worcester, with a quittance of Falconer for the purchase of Davington; and another of Roys for the purchase of Titchwell. Ask my cousin, Henry Sturmer's wife, to search for an indenture and other writings between me and Sellyng or Lady Wiltshire. As you inform me that Sir Thomas Tuddenham has sent to John Clerk to be at London, you must ask him and his wife to go before the bailiffs at Yarmouth, and certify how it was that Bishop's wife did not receive the £100 I was ordered to pay her. John Clerk must not come up [to London] till I send for him.

Special labour has been made that Justice Yelverton should not come down [into Norfolk] this Martinmas, but the King and the Lords have determined he shall keep his day, and the labour that ye, with my cousin Paston, made of late to my Lord Norfolk was right well advised, in case that the [visit of the] Justice should be countermanded. Urge my friends to do their very best for me now in the matters laboured last at the oyer and terminer [assizes], that they may take a worshipful end.

Thank Nicholas Bokking for what he did about the certificate of the jury in the enquiry about Titchwell, and beg him to get it sealed in time, which will be a great evidence for the recovery of my manor.... Send for William Cole about the accounts and thank the Parson of Hellesden for the three writings of Wiltshire's will...sent me by Worcester, but say I prayed him to search for more.

A considerable number of similar letters have survived, all testifying to the old knight's remarkable grasp of his affairs. He never seems at a loss for a fact, or where the evidence to support it is to be found, and never forgets an injury done him or a debt left unpaid. Nothing is too small to attract his notice. Only four years before his death, at the age of seventy-seven, he writes to John Paston saying that he hears that Paston was at a dinner in

Norwich where 'scornful language' was uttered against him in this wise.

> Ware thee, cousin, ware;
> Go we to dinner; go we where?
> To Sir John Fastolf—and there
> We shall well pay therefore.

What the meaning was [he adds] I know well to no good intent to me ward; wherefore, cousin, I pray you, as my trust is in you, that ye give me knowledge by writing what gentlemen they be that had this report...and what more gentlemen were present, as ye would I should (and were my duty to do for you) in semblable wise. And I shall keep your information in this matter secret, and with God's grace, so privy for them as they shall not all be well pleased!

Such a touchy nature, combined with the inevitable business and legal operations connected with his many properties, kept Fastolf constantly engaged in the courts. He writes incessantly to his many agents in London and in the counties where he was a landowner, urging them to sterner courses, suggesting methods which may serve his ends—not always above suspicion—as when he writes: 'Labour to the Sheriff for the return of such panels as will speak for me'; or: 'Entreat the Sheriff as well as ye can by reasonable rewards, rather than fail.' He does not hesitate to write to one of the justices asking him to favour the cause of his agent, although this does not prevent him from protesting energetically against unlawful practices on the part of others.

Life for those employed by him must have been hard, and as the years went on he seems to have grown more and more exacting. One of his chief agents was Thomas Howes, parson of Castle Combe, a living within Fastolf's gift. Characteristically he bestowed this on Howes as a means of endowing him, and then proceeded to use him as his agent, so that he was seldom in his parish, but was kept on the move from place to place, inspecting, bullying and reporting according to his master's orders. His every move was watched, and a false step could produce from Fastolf a reproof as follows:

> Right trusty friend, I greet you well, and wish you to know that I find it very strange...that you have mentioned me and said to John Andrews of Ipswich, in the presence of divers men, that you have sufficient warrants, written and sealed by me, to indemnify you, in case you are condemned to pay the sum Andrews sues you for. Know for certain no such warrant has passed my seal: neither did I command you to do anything that should be against the law or against right and truth.... And therefore I ought not, nor will not, pay for you.

Howes was not alone among those who served him who tasted constantly of his temper. One of them, Henry Windsor, briefly summed up his opinion of his master by saying: 'It is not unknown that cruel and vengeful he hath ever been, and for the most part without pity and mercy.' William Worcester, a much more important figure, who acted as his secretary for many years, had entered Fastolf's service in 1436, and some twenty years later was complaining that he existed '*inter egenos ut servus ad aratrum* (among the destitute, as a serf at the plough)'. In answer to his pleas for better treatment all he got from Fastolf was that he wished Worcester had been a priest, since then he could have presented him to one of the livings in his gift! No wonder that Worcester writes on another occasion: 'God give him grace of a good wholesome counsel and of a good disposition; *non est opus unius diei, nec unius septimanæ*' (it will take more than one day—or one week for the matter of that—[to amend Fastolf's temper]).

Even to those of his own kin he was far from generous. Stephen Scrope, his stepson, got little sympathy from him, for among other profitable ways of money-making Fastolf did not forget the lucrative business of buying and selling of wardships; and, since Stephen was his ward, soon after his marriage, Fastolf handed him over to Chief Justice Gascoigne for the sum of 500 marks, with the intention of marrying him to one of Gascoigne's daughters. Scrope went to live in the household of Gascoigne where he was very unhappy and contracted a sickness that was with him for some thirteen or fourteen years. Some hitch occurred in the marriage plans, and Gascoigne went back on his word, apparently, and proposed to marry Scrope to a girl of lesser social position. Such a marriage, said Scrope's friends, would 'disparage' the young man, and they prevailed on Fastolf to buy him back again for the sum which Gascoigne had originally paid. Scrope bitterly resented all this. 'He bought me and sold me as a beast, against all right and law, to mine hurt more than a thousand marks', he wrote later, 'through the which I took a sickness...whereby I am disfigured in my person and shall be while I live.'

Fastolf had also seriously impaired Scrope's position, for soon after his marriage, his wife Milicent entailed all her estates on Fastolf, thus depriving Scrope of his inheritance which an earlier deed (1390) between Milicent and her first husband had secured for him. This manœuvre left Scrope a poor man dependent on his stepfather's generosity, and for the rest of his life he had to watch Fastolf battening on his manors, and but grudgingly helping him. For the time being he apparently lived as best he might, but about 1421–4 Scrope determined to enter the service of Humphrey, duke of Gloucester, and to seek his fortunes with him. To this end he sold some manors for 500 marks, but when Fastolf heard of this, he wrote to Milicent urging her to persuade Scrope to join him in France, which he eventually did, and served with his stepfather for some years. But in time this arrangement wore thin: a dispute arising between Scrope and the marshal of Harfleur, Fastolf took the latter's part, and Scrope returned to live with his mother in England.

Fastolf followed this up first by writing to say that Scrope must pay for his own maintenance, and later by refusing to give him an allowance so that he could enter the service of the duke of Gloucester. Fastolf invited him to return and serve under him in France again, or if he could find for himself a suitable wife, Fastolf promised to do by him as he should, in such a fashion as Scrope would be content. This latter proposition attracted Scrope, and a little later, about 1433, he married, and Fastolf granted him a Yorkshire manor but little else in the way of livelihood, and this little he withdrew after a while. By this time Scrope had children and other responsibilities, and after living in poverty for three years he was forced to do what had been done to him—to sell his daughter as a ward! 'For very need', he writes, 'I was fain to sell a little daughter I have for much less than I should have done by possibility'—part of his complaint evidently being the lowness of the price he got for the child. Her wardship went to a knight whose name remains unknown and Scrope, who was now a widower, began to look about for a marriage which would better his position. After some time, about 1454, he married Joan, daughter of Sir Richard Bingham, a justice of the King's Bench, but so miserable was his condition that the justice interceded on his behalf with Fastolf to allow him to enjoy a manor which was part of the Scrope inheritance, but little seems to have come of this, and the negotiations were still in progress when Fastolf died in 1459. By this time Scrope was over sixty, and had but few years to enjoy the inheritance which Fastolf had kept from him for so long.

To turn to more pleasant aspects of his character; Fastolf was a faithful son of the Church, and was a generous benefactor. Not only did he hope (as we shall see later) to leave behind him a religious foundation, endowed by himself, but he gave liberally to ecclesiastical bodies during his lifetime. Thomas Howes is said to have dispensed £4000 on his master's behalf for such purposes, while from time to time we hear of Fastolf's paying for a new window, or that he has made a loan to an impoverished abbey. Near at hand, the Abbey of St Benet's at Holm—the oldest religious foundation in Norfolk, whose towers would have been visible from the rising ground at Caister—was generously helped by Fastolf, who paid for the rebuilding of the south aisle of the church, and for the erection of a new chapel, both in freestone.

He seems also to have had some interest in things of the mind, for at the time of his death there were at least twenty volumes in French found at Caister. Among them were the Bible, the encyclopædia of Bartholomew the Englishman, the *Chronicles of England and France*; a number of religious works, including *Vices and Vertues*, and the *Meditations of St Bernard*, and also *Vegetius on Chivalry* and the *Roman de la Rose*. We also know that he had some

English books, for at the end of *The Dicts and Sayings of the Philosophers* we read that it was translated out of French for the 'contemplacion and solace' of Fastolf, as was Cicero's *De Senectute*, and probably one or two other works. Like many well-to-do men of his time Fastolf evidently kept a small library of books from which extracts could be read to him when he so desired, and from which he could derive moral comfort, information and delight.

As befitted a great soldier and landowner, Fastolf lived in considerable style. In Southwark, as well as in Norfolk and Wiltshire, he had fine houses, and a large body of servants to attend on him and his family. In 1446 he obtained possession of five houses in St Olave's, Southwark, and had also a good deal of other property in Southwark. His own residence—Fastolf's Place—went by this name for 200 years after his death, although it narrowly escaped being burnt down in 1450 by Jack Cade and the Kentish rebels. When Fastolf learnt that Cade was encamped on Blackheath he sent one of his retainers, John Payn, to find out what were the demands of the insurgents. Payn, attended by a man with two horses, rode into Cade's camp, and was promptly arrested. The servant with the horses galloped off, but Payn was brought before Cade, who asked him what was his business and why he had sent away the horses with such haste. Payn equivocated, but was soon recognized as one of Fastolf's retainers. On this a cry of treason was raised, and Payn accompanied by a herald was sent to the four quarters of the camp, and there proclaimed as one sent to spy on them by the greatest traitor in England and France, Sir John Fastolf, who had reduced the garrisons in France and so lost the king's possessions overseas. Furthermore, it was proclained that Fastolf had garrisoned his house in Southwark with old soldiers back from the wars, who would destroy Cade and his men when they marched into Southwark.

There was only one penalty for such an emissary—the block, and Payn was brought to Cade's tent, where axe and block were brought forth, but fortunately his life was saved by Cade's sword-bearer and carver, who said that a hundred or more would die if Payn were executed. He was released on oath that he would go to Southwark, fetch his arms and return to help them. He took with him to Fastolf a statement of the rebel's demands, at the same time advising him to put up no resistance at Southwark, but to retire to the Tower with his men. Fastolf did so, leaving only two men behind him, and when the rebels reached Southwark, Payn had great difficulty in preventing them from firing the place. He calmed them down, and entertained them with meat and drink, and in time they withdrew, taking him with them, and later on putting him in the front of the affray on London Bridge where he fought for six hours and was seriously wounded.

Outside London, Fastolf spent most of his time in Norfolk where he had a number of houses. In Norwich as in Southwark the family house was known as Fastolf's Place, and its rooms were adorned with wooden effigies of saints and other figures, sacred and profane. At Yarmouth he also had property, but it was his birthplace, Caister, just outside Yarmouth, that was dearest to him. An account book of 1431–2 shows that while he was in France his wife lived there with his sister Margaret, wife of one of his lieutenants, and also with a cousin of the family, attended by officials of the household, and a chaplain as well as by a domestic staff some twenty in number—cooks, bakers, pantry-men, gardener, fisherman and dairy maid.

For many years, however, the idea of building a magnificent family home at Caister had been in Fastolf's mind. As early as the reign of Henry V, it is said, he began planning to this end, and by the time of his final return to England the work was in hand, but it was making slow progress, and in October 1443 Fastolf obtained a licence from the Crown to use six ships entirely for the purpose of bringing building materials to Yarmouth. They were not to be commandeered by the king's purveyors, and nothing short of a national emergency was to divert them from their purpose.

Progress, however, was slow, for the whole was planned on a magnificent scale. The great walls with their battlements, pierced with loopholes for defence, have mostly crumbled away, together with the great tower which still was ninety feet high within living memory, although unsafe and the haunt of jackdaws. The grand design made provision for at least twenty-six chambers, in addition to the chapel, public rooms and offices, the whole area of the site covering some six acres. One of the chambers—that for Lady Milicent, Fastolf's wife—she never lived to occupy, for it was not until eight years after her death, that Fastolf first came into residence in the autumn of 1454. Here were accumulated the treasures of a long life—furniture, gold and silver plate and cups, tapestries, household stuff of all kinds in great quantity. To take a glance at one item only—tapestries. These hangings were very popular in the Middle Ages, and were widely used as decorations and to cover the bare walls. Originally made around Arras—whence the common name for them of 'Arras cloths'—their manufacture had become a great industry there and in north-east France, and some of the most talented craftsmen spent their lives in producing these lovely and elaborate pieces, which now we see, robbed by injurious time of their first splendour, only in museums and show places. Fastolf, like all rich men, had tapestries in number—religious pieces, showing the Adoration of the Shepherds, or the Assumption of Our Lady; sporting scenes of men shooting ducks with a cross-bow, or of a huntsman in a blue and red hood, hunting the boar; martial scenes, as in the great tapestry depicting the siege of Falaise, in which he had taken part, etc. Other tapestry cloths did not hang on the walls, but covered benches in the halls, or were made into coverlets for the beds.

Amidst all this splendour the old man's days were running out. The year he moved to Caister it was certified by the official concerned that Fastolf was unable to attend the annual meeting of the Knights of the Garter since 'he could neither go nor ride without danger to health', and he never attended again. Indeed, it is doubtful if he ever was far from Caister once he had removed there. He was an old tired man. His friends and servants found him harder than ever to please. John Paston was the confidant of many of them, who poured out their grievances to him in unguarded phrases which bespeak their irritation.

At reverence of God [writes one of them] be as soon as ye may with my master to ease his spirits. He questions and disputes with his servants here, and sometimes will not be answered nor satisfied but according to his wilfulness, for it suffices not our simple wits to appease his soul. But when he speaks with Master Yelverton, you, or with William Jenny, and such others as be authorized in the law, and with abundance of goods, he is content, and he is pleased with your answers and motions, as reason is that he be. So would Jesus that one of you three, or some such other in your stead, might hang at his girdle daily to answer his matters.

Among these matters two things in particular occupied Sir John's mind in his latest years—first, the debts owing to him, and secondly, the wish he had to found a religious college at Caister. The subject of the many sums owing to him for his services in France and his various loans to the Crown is a recurrent theme, and he made a vigorous attempt in 1455 to come to a final settlement of the matter. No less than four drafts of his claims against the Crown survive. These extended back to his early service in Guienne in the reign of Henry IV, and include claims for ransom of prisoners, charges met by Fastolf on the king's behalf as captain or lieutenant of lands and castles overseas. Loans to the king to help send forces to France; wages of himself and his troops unpaid; wrongful eviction from manors, 'great oppressions, grievous and outrageous amerciaments, and many great, horrible extortions', etc. —all help to swell the bill of some £14,000 alleged to be owing to him. As far as we know, they were still outstanding at the time of his death, and what part of them was really justifiable and what part not, is beyond our finding out. Certainly he was deprived of the ransom of two prisoners at least, and there is no doubt that he lent considerable sums to the Crown which seem never to have been repaid.

Fastolf used this as an argument when trying to establish

his religious foundation or college. He wished to set up at Caister a college, consisting of a prior and six monks of the Order of St Benedict, together with seven poor men, 'to pray for my soul, and for the souls of my father and mother, and of all my kinsfolk...and for all Christian souls, therefore to sing and say daily divine service and prayers in perpetuity'. When he learned of certain difficulties raised by Crown officials he appealed for consideration in recompense of his 'long service continued and done unto the King, and to his noble father...and never yet guerdoned or rewarded'. Here again, Fastolf was unlucky. He died without seeing his college established, and indeed after some hesitancy, the scheme was abandoned, although Fastolf was so determined on it that he left Paston instructions in his will to tear the whole castle down if anyone sought to take it from him and use it for any other purpose.

Into all this, however, we need not go. Fastolf died as he had lived—a hard, determined man who in a long life had had opportunity to show a many-sided character not ill suited to the changing, troubled days through which he lived.

THOMAS HOCCLEVE

The labours of generations of Chaucerian scholars have brought to light much information concerning the poet's official life as a servant of the Crown. His services at home and abroad are entered in the public records, and from them a fairly complete account of how his career shaped itself can be seen. But none of these records shows so much of the man as do the revealing lines, written by himself, in *The Hous of Fame*, in which we see him in his little chamber in Aldgate Tower, hearing nothing of what was going on unless his neighbours told it to him, since as his interlocutor says:

> when thy labour doon al ys,
> And hast mad alle thy rekenynges,
> In stede of reste and newe thynges,
> Thou goost hom to thy hous anoon;
> And, also domb as any stoon,
> Thou sittest at another book
> Tyl fully daswed ys thy look,
> And lyvest thus as an heremyte.

Here, forgetting the turmoil of the wharves, where he laboured as the controller of customs and subsidy of wools, skins and hides, and according to the terms of his appointment wrote the rolls with his own hand—here he was able to read and to write, with nothing to interrupt him as evening wore on till the curfew sounded from Bow Church, and

> The warden of the yates gan to calle
> The folk which that without the yates were,
> And bad hem driven in hire bestes alle,
> Or al the nyght they moste bleven there.
>
> *bleven:* remain.

Meanwhile Chaucer read on in his beloved books—his old friends Virgil and Ovid; his newly acquired Dante and Boccaccio; and the French poetry past or present of *The Romance of the Rose*, or that of Machaut, Froissart or Deschamps.

Unlike Deschamps, alas, Chaucer does not constantly allow his own likes and dislikes or other personal matters to creep into his poems, and we must be content with this one glimpse of the poet *en pantoufles*. Nor do his contemporaries Langland and Gower. Langland (if we may take Long Will to be the poet) in the course of his poem gives us a few hints of himself—of his schooling and education, or of his unsatisfying life in London, but little enough. Gower, in the course of his voluminous works in Latin and French, shows himself alarmed and critical of the way things are going in the world about him. His most graphic autobiographical moment comes when he tells us how he met Richard II in his barge on the Thames, and being welcomed aboard, was cross-questioned by the king about his writings, and as a result was commanded to write 'som newe thing'—the outcome being his English poem, the *Confessio Amantis*.

Thomas Hoccleve

In the fifteenth century writers were a little more informative. The two leading poets of the century, Lydgate and Hoccleve, talk of themselves from time to time, while lesser men, such as Bokenham, Shirley, Ashby or Hawes, tell us something of their hopes and fears as poets and of their reasons for writing. Outstanding amongst all these was Thomas Hoccleve, whose poems were written in the first quarter of the fifteenth century.

Hoccleve is a good example of something which only recently had come into the world of letters—a man who had a secular profession or calling which took up the main part of his time, and who worked at his poetry only in his leisure. Chaucer's output as a poet is so considerable and so assured in its manner that we are apt to forget that it is the spare-time occupation of one who in his time was ambassador, controller of customs, clerk of the royal works, knight of the shire and much else besides. Hoccleve, his pupil and disciple, could make no claims such as these, for he had only one position all his life, but he too, like Chaucer, employed part of his leisure in the writing of poetry. That it was poetry of not a very high class need not concern us here: our interest in his versifying is for the light which it throws on his life as a professional man by day, and a man of letters by night, so to speak.

The bare outline of Hoccleve's life is soon told. As a young man he entered the office of the Privy Seal. There he spent his working life for some thirty-six years. From time to time in his leisure hours he wrote verses which he dedicated to influential members of the court. He lived a reckless life as a bachelor, but about the year 1410 or 1411 married, and in due course was retired on a pension. That is all: but behind this lies the story of a fifteenth-century civil servant and man of letters which enables us to see something of the personal history of one who at first sight appears to be no more than a necessary drudge—a black-coated worker of the Middle Ages.

Of Hoccleve's life before he went to the Privy Seal office we know nothing. We must assume, however, that in his native village in Bedfordshire or elsewhere he had acquired sufficient learning to enable him to deal with the work of his office, and undoubtedly the fundamental necessity there was a competent knowledge of Latin. This, in common with thousands of other boys in England and western Europe, he painfully acquired by many years of study. Every village priest was a potential elementary schoolmaster, and Hoccleve may have learnt his letters from him or perhaps from one of his assistants—the holy-water carrier—who strove to instruct the abler children in the alphabet, in the elements of reading and later in the mysteries of song—in so far as these were required for the decent performance of the daily services. Throughout England in the Middle Ages such instruction was being given: here well done, here indifferently, here not at all. But the possibility was always there. Even though such a disgrace as Langland's 'Sloth the Parson' held the living for a time, there was always the chance that his successor would be as worthy as Chaucer's 'poor person'—and so it went on.

The young Hoccleve's ability, we may imagine, was early observed, and from the elementary or 'petty' school, he would be advanced step by step, as we see were the children in the school in *The Prioresses Tale*, ostensibly 'in Asia', but in reality in any English town. There, it will be remembered, were

> Children an heep, ycomen of Cristen blood,
> That lerned in that scole yeer by yere
> Swich manere doctrine as men usen there,
> That is to seyn, to syngen and to rede,
> As smale children doon in hire childhede.

The poem goes on to tell us of the various classes in the school. The 'litel clergeon, seven yeer of age' is seen learning to read when in another class he hears the elder boys singing the Latin anthem *Alma redemptoris mater*. He asks a boy in a higher class to tell him what the words meant, but his companion cannot do so, for he is not yet a student of Latin but is still learning to sing, and has not yet to bother about the meaning of what he sings. That will come later; for, as he says, 'I lerne song, I kan but smal grammeere'.

Grammar, that is the study of Latin, only began when the boy could read and write competently in the vernacular. Once this was accomplished, the tedious and painful business of learning the rules of accidence, simple syntax and the formation of easy sentences began. Hoccleve, like other boys, would have taken down on his tablets words and phrases dictated to him by his master, and in time would have been able to repeat by heart the preterites, supines, etc., and to have posed his fellows with these and other grammatical points at times devoted to this purpose. The study of grammars and works such as those of Donatus, or Alexander de Villa Dei, was succeeded by the reading of selected passages from Cato and Seneca, Horace, Ovid and Virgil. Side by side with this went the writing of Latin, gradually working up to the production of exercises in which the graces of rhetorical ornament and the rigorous clarity of logical argument were displayed. If they were not, it was not for want of effort on the master's part, constantly reinforced by the use of the rod, for beating was an inseparable part of all medieval education, and the constant application of the birch for all offences however trivial was axiomatic.

Hoccleve, like all other schoolboys of his day, would have enjoyed reciting the rigorous verses of an anonymous writer

Hay, hay, by this day,
What vayleth it me thowgh I say nay?

[1]

I wold fayn be a clarke,
But yet hit is a strange werke;
The byrchyn twygges be so sharpe
Hit makith me have a faynt harte;
What vayleth it me thowgh I say nay?

[2]

On Monday in the mornyng whan I shall rise,
At vi of the clok, hyt is the gise,
To go to skole without avise,
I had lever go twenti myle twyse;
What vayleth it me thowgh I say nay?

[3]

My master lokith as he were madde:
'Wher hast thou be, thou sory ladde?'
'Milked dukkes, my moder badde.'
Hit was no mervayle thow I were sadde;
What vayleth it me thowgh I say nay?

[4]

My master pepered my ars with well good spede;
Hit was worse than fynkyll sede;
He wold not leve till it did blede;
Mych sorow have he for his dede!
   What vayleth it me thowgh I say nay?

[5]

I wold my master were a watt,
And my boke a wyld catt,
And a brase of grehowndes in his toppe;
I wold be glade for to se that.
   What vayleth it me thowgh I say nay?

[6]

I wold my master were an hare,
And all his bokes houndes were,
And I myself a joly hontere;
To blow my horn I wold not spare,
For if he were dede I wold not care.
   What vayleth it me thowgh I say nay?

avise: argument. *fynkyll*: fennel. *watt*: hare. *top*: fore-lock.

Side by side with his study of Latin, Hoccleve was also acquiring French in all probability, for his future career demanded a working knowledge of both languages, since the documents issued by the Privy Seal were as often written in French as in Latin. Furthermore, French was still in use amongst the aristocratic and learned classes in England, and some schoolmasters still taught Latin by means of French, although the practice was fast dying out in Hoccleve's youth, as was the use of French itself. At the same time it was realized that ignorance of French was a disadvantage—especially for one like Hoccleve whose future was to lie in official circles.

Whether or no Hoccleve went straight into the Privy Seal office from school we cannot tell. It is just possible that before doing so he spent some time at one of the Inns of Chancery, for we learn from the great fifteenth-century lawyer, Sir John Fortescue, that students entered one of these Inns of Chancery where 'they study the nature of *Original* and *Judicial Writs*, which are the very first principles of the law', and he goes on to call the Inns 'a sort of academy or gymnasium, fit for persons of their station; where they learn singing, and all kinds of music, dancing and such other accomplishments and diversions as are suitable to their quality'. In fact, the training in the Inns was on a liberal basis, and instruction in Latin, French History, music and other subjects was available. They were admirable finishing schools for any professional man, and one of these—Chester's Inn, in the Strand—may well have attracted Hoccleve, for from 1377 to 1381 it appears to have housed the keeper of the Privy Seal and his clerks.

When Hoccleve entered the Privy Seal as a young man of eighteen or nineteen, he found himself in one of the busiest offices of the day, for by this time the Privy Seal had established itself after the Exchequer and the Great Wardrobe as the third office of state. Moreover, by the comparative simplicity of its rules, and the quickness with which it functioned, it was more and more used, not only by the king and his servants, but also by many suitors to the Crown. It could issue warrants and writs, or could order men to appear before the king's council. It sent out letters of summons to Parliament; it gave instructions to the king's officers, agents or servants at home or abroad; it issued pardons, licences, grants, safe-conducts—in short the office was kept very fully employed by the mass of business which constantly came before it.

Now such a variety of affairs could not be mastered in a day, and experience had shown that a man had to serve for some while as an apprentice or learner before he could be given full responsibility. Many years after he had entered the Privy Seal we find that Hoccleve had attached to him a certain John Welde, who was probably being trained by him to become one of the senior members of the staff who were known as the clerks of the Privy Seal. We may imagine that Hoccleve went through some such preliminary training, but it could not have been long, for he soon is described by the official title 'clerc en l'offise du prive seal'. There he was to remain for some thirty-six years; and, as was the lot of most of his colleagues, he might never have attracted further notice but for the fact that he combined a literary life with his official life, and at times talked about himself rather than about his poetic subject—to our great benefit.

At this time the Privy Seal office was situated near the Palace of Westminster. We know little about it physically. From various sources we read of the provision of 'a green cloth for the table of the privy seal', of a calculating table, of two forms and of chests in which documents could be kept—little enough to help us envisage the room in which Hoccleve and his fellow clerks, together with their assistants and 'writing clerks', spent their days. How many there were in all it is impossible to say. For instance, the number of senior clerks varied: we hear of four in the late fourteenth century and again in 1444, but in the early years of the fifteenth century the number had risen to nine for a while. Much of the work was of a routine nature, and once the technical details (which were considerable) had been mastered by the assistant and writing clerks, they could be left to get on with the semi-mechanical job of writing out the documents, while Hoccleve and his fellows gave their attention to more difficult problems. As an aid to the office during his time there, Hoccleve compiled a large book of formularies and precedents to enable those less experienced than himself to see how to draw up the various kinds of documents. Nevertheless, even senior clerks like himself could not escape a good deal of drudgery, and, after some years at the work, Hoccleve complained that it was not only boring and exhausting, but actually injurious to health. Twenty years bent over his desk convinced Hoccleve that those who thought such work child's play did not know what they were talking about. 'Let them try', he says, 'they will soon learn otherwise. Some workmen can sing, talk, or tell tales: some make jokes and thus help to pass the time happily enough. For the scribe it is different. He must concentrate on what he is doing. His eye and his hand work together to put on to paper that which his mind dictates:

> A writer mot thre thynges to hym knytte,
> And in tho may be no disseuerance;
> Mynde, ee, and hand—non may fro other flitte,
> But in them mot be joynt contynuance.

As a result his health suffers. Few people realize how bending for hours over the parchment sorely cramps the stomach and grievously strains the back. Furthermore, the eyes are injured by continuously looking at the white surface (Hoccleve admits elsewhere that he ought to wear spectacles but he is too vain), more so than by any other craft. In short, the whole body suffers as the scribes 'stoupe and stare upon the shepes skyn'.

So thinks Hoccleve, as he looks back on his work at the office, and perhaps it was just as well that he did not realize that he was then only two-thirds of the way through his professional career, although he must have known how difficult it was to get promotion to a better position or to another sort of life. Around him in the office were others of long service: there were William Flete and John Heath, who had joined the office at much the same time as himself, while his friend John Bailay was only a year his junior. William Dighton who retired a few years after Hoccleve entered on his duties had served for thirty-eight years, and another of his contemporaries also had long service to his credit.

In short, Hoccleve was one of the many minor officials in medieval England who could not expect much in the way of change. The patronage that the keeper had at his disposal was small. Only the king was able to help, and an insignificant clerk of his Privy Seal had little to hope for save a sop from time to time in the shape of an outlaw's goods, or some minor property that came into the king's hands. This, no doubt, was welcome, for his emoluments were both uncertain in kind and amount, and irregular in payment. These emoluments were generally of two kinds: wages in actual cash, which were usually small; and allowances which took the form of robes, perquisites, food and lodging. In earlier days the clerks had formed part of the royal household, and were suitably fed and maintained there: but, by the end of the fourteenth century, they lived away from the court (*extra curiam*), and the keeper was allowed twenty shillings a day for his staff. Early in the fifteenth century it was seen that this was not enough (it is even suggested that it all went to the keeper as his fee) and henceforth a number of Middlesex manors were set aside to provide for the keeper and his staff, not by way of wages, but for their maintenance, since they were not living under the king's roof.

So far as wages are concerned, in Hoccleve's time it had become usual for a clerk to draw 7½*d.* a day after he had acquired some competence at his work. In the course of time—usually not less than ten years—his services might be recognized by an exchequer grant or annuity of £10 per annum, and this is what was awarded to Hoccleve by Henry IV on 12 November 1399. The deed states that the grant is made for good and laudable service in the Privy Seal office, and is to be paid in two parts at Easter and Michaelmas for the rest of his life, unless he is promoted to a benefice, without cure of souls, worth £20 a year. He was comparatively lucky, for one of his colleagues, Richard Prior, had to serve for twenty years before any permanent grant was made to him. However, ten or twelve years' service seems to have been the usual period at the end of which it was possible for a clerk to petition the king for an award. Hoccleve's annuity was raised to £13. 6*s.* 8*d.* after he had completed about twenty years' service, and it remained at this figure until he retired.

It will have been observed that his first annuity was given him for life, with the proviso that it would lapse should he be promoted to a benefice, without cure of souls, worth £20 a year. This was the prize for ever dangling before the eyes of the hard-worked clerk. There was always the hope of being appointed to a sinecure which would help him to pay his way without any tiresome conditions of residence or the conduct of services which would interfere with the holding of his clerkship. It required a very substantial living to persuade a man to surrender his civil for an ecclesiastical appointment. What most hoped to do was to remain in London and at the same time, as some of Hoccleve's colleagues were doing, to draw a steady income from some country living. Thus, Lawrence Bailay was the rector of two Yorkshire parishes, while William Donne was the warden of an hospital in one diocese, and a rector in another. Their colleague, John Wellingborough, was a rector in Lincolnshire, a warden in Dorset and also a prebendary of no less than four other churches. Such men could afford to regard their official salary with comparative indifference.

Not so Hoccleve, however, who never received any such preferment, and who again and again tells us that his 'rentes' did not exceed £4 a year in addition to his annuity, and he was ever in fear lest this annuity should be withdrawn or remain unpaid.

Indeed, it was the uncertainty whether or no they would be paid that constantly beset Hoccleve and his fellows. The Exchequer of the Middle Ages was often in lack of funds; we hear of the king pledging the royal jewels, or borrowing from ecclesiastical or lay lords from time to time in order to make ends meet. An empty chest left everyone anxious: Hoccleve on occasion appeals to anyone whom he thinks can help—Prince Henry, the chancellor, the treasurer, influential friends—and not without reason for, as we can see from the official records, his annuity was frequently overdue. This is borne out by his poems: he writes a 'balade to my Lord the Chancellor', asking for a writ ordering the Exchequer to pay him his arrears, or another to the under-treasurer, Henry Somer, in which he plays upon his name, saying that as the summer season brings forth its bounteous fruits, so he hopes that Somer will bring to him and his fellow clerks their Michaelmas annuity. To this end they all pray:

> Hasteth our harvest, as soon as ye may!
> For fere of stormes our wit is aweye;
> Were our seed inned, wel we mighten pleye.

He even flies higher, and asks Henry V, 'victorious kyng', to give the clerks of the Privy Seal some money, or they will have to 'trotte unto Newgate'. Their demands, he reminds the king, are not excessive or outrageous, and they have worked long and hard, early and late have been liege men to their 'worthy Prince, mirrour of prowesse!' Earlier than this, while Henry was still Prince of Wales, Hoccleve had addressed to him a similar petition:

> My yeerly guerdoun, myn annuite,
> That was me graunted for my long labour,
> Is al behynde, I may naght payed be.

and elsewhere in the same poem he harps on his arrears and what difficulty he has to get them paid.

Hoccleve was not solely dependent on his wages, however, for by tradition the clerks were accustomed to receive two yearly robes, one for the summer valued at 20*s*., while a more substantial winter robe was worth 26*s*. 8*d*. Then there were other perquisites. From time to time some outlaw's goods were handed over to the clerks who sold them for what they would fetch, as did Hoccleve and three of his friends in 1395, when they received goods to the value of £40. Hoccleve's fellow, Robert Fry, was even more fortunate, for in 1401 he was granted an annual income of £6. 13*s.* 4*d.* from the lands of an outlaw, while another of Hoccleve's colleagues was given the rents of two shops in the Shambles to the value of £10 per annum. Lower down the office scale, one of Hoccleve's assistants was given a smaller grant of 26*s.* 8*d.* a year, and so on. While these rewards were uncertain in amount and sporadic in appearance, and moreover were solely a matter of grace, they seem to have occurred sufficiently often to keep those concerned expectant and reasonably content.

More important, perhaps, because much more frequent were the tips expected by the clerks when they wrote out the letter of Privy Seal asked for by some private person. Unfortunately for the clerks, however, such persons often sent their servants to sue out the writ, and these men, Hoccleve complains, took for themselves the fee that by rights should have come to the clerks. Their trick was to collect the writ, and to tell Hoccleve and his friends not to fear, for their lord should thank them another day; and furthermore to hint that he had the ear of the king, and would speak for them should they need a royal favour. 'It is of no use to complain', Hoccleve says, 'for it is the servant's version of the story that will be believed, and often the writ is not for their master at all, but has been obtained under his name for another of whom he knows nothing.' Whatever happens the clerks stand to lose: whoever gets the writ in these circumstances, they get nothing. Not all lords' men play them such scurvy tricks, Hoccleve admits, but there are 'ful many swych', and the result is that the clerks lose both thanks and fees, and also get a bad name: 'God geve hem sorowe that so with us pleye.'

Other 'rewards' occasionally came the way of the

clerks, often as a recompense for extra or unusual work. John Burgh, for example, was taken in the train of the Lord Treasurer on one of his official tours, and received £6. 13*s*. 4*d*. for the fortnight he and his valet were away from home. On another occasion six of the clerks were given £2 as a reward for writing copies of divers truces for the information of our ambassadors to France—perhaps a task done out of office hours. For a last example we may note that John Welde bought sixty-six sheets of parchment at a shilling a sheet upon which to write a Bible for the king.

In addition to these various sources of income, the unmarried clerks were found lodgings at the king's expense. Many of the bishops had large London houses which they only fully occupied at intervals, and were glad to let them out from time to time. It was in such a hostel that Hoccleve and his fellows lived—the residence of the bishop of Lichfield or Chester, known as Chester's Inn, which stood near the church of St Mary le Strand, at the east end of the Strand, and from here, by boat or by road, the clerks went to their office at Westminster.

This then was his position as Hoccleve summed it up half-way through his career. He had a roof over his head and a permanent source of employment. His work was monotonous, arduous, and as he thought, prejudicial to health, and he hoped to escape from it. In the meantime he had an annuity (which he would have liked better had it been paid more regularly), winter and summer robes, fees, pickings and occasional 'rewards', the cash value of the last three items being estimated by Hoccleve to be some £4 (six marks) a year. In his more responsible moments he must have realized that his lot was a reasonably satisfactory one. His total emoluments compared favourably with those of many of the clergy, for example. The average annual value of eighteen Bristol livings at this time was £11. 7*s.* 0*d.*—a higher figure than that in most parts of the country—while Hoccleve's emoluments must have been about £20 per annum.

So far we have been mainly concerned with Hoccleve's official career. Thanks to his writings, however, we know much about him both as a person and as a poet. It must be confessed that he had no very high ideals concerning his poetry. He used what meagre poetic gifts he had mainly for one purpose—that of augmenting his finances. We have already seen how he asks various officials to help him to secure payment of his annuity by writing them 'balades'; and although unlike his contemporary Lydgate he does not directly ask his patrons for money, a glance at the names of those to whom he dedicates his verses betrays his purpose. It was, presumably, through his official position that he came into touch with many of these. He seems to have known Henry V, both as Prince of Wales and as King, and he translated the *De Regimine Principum* of Aegidius Romanus for Henry in 1411–12. As we shall see, in 1421 he translated another work for Duke Humphrey, while among members of the nobility with whom he was in contact were the duke of Bedford and the duke of York; the latter, Hoccleve tells us, having once asked him to send copies of all the *Balades* he had by him. Further patrons were the duchess of York, the Lord Chancellor, the countess of Westmorland and Lady Hereford as well as a number of lesser folk.

As an example of Hoccleve's care in trying to make his

poem acceptable to his patron we may take his translation of a story from the great medieval collection known as the *Gesta Romanorum*—the tale of the Emperor Jereslaus and his loving and faithful wife. Hoccleve tells his friend that he has long promised to write a book for Duke Humphrey. He first thought of translating the famous work of Vegetius on chivalry and the art of war, but Humphrey knows all this, and his recent feats at Cherbourg and at Rouen bear witness to his valour. He does not know what to write and appeals to his friend for advice. 'Does it matter on what subject you write?' his friend asks. 'No', says Hoccleve, 'so that it be mateere of honestee.' At that, he is advised to write a poem in praise of women. His friend reminds him, despite Hoccleve's protestations, that he has often blamed women and that they have a grudge against him. 'Write now in their favour', he urges, 'and you will do well. The Duke loves the company of ladies, and will show them your book, and thus you will please him, and also win their forgiveness.' Hoccleve declares that he has been misunderstood, but on reflection decides to accept the advice, and to please the ladies sets to work to translate the story of how Jereslaus's wife remained faithful to him, despite the most daunting circumstances.

Now while we need not believe every word of this circumstantial narrative to be true, it probably indicates fairly enough the kind of thoughts that were passing through the author's mind as he contemplated his long-promised poem to the rich and powerful Humphrey, duke of Gloucester. We have only to recall Humphrey's reputation as the most generous of patrons, to put two and two together, to see what was going on.

Hoccleve's lack of funds was always in his mind. In his verse translation entitled *The Regement of Princes*, that is, how rulers should be governed, in the course of a two-thousand word prologue the theme constantly recurs. This is understandable, since the whole affair is largely autobiographical, but when he turns to the actual translation which he dedicates to the prince of Wales he continues to harp on his own troubles. When he writes of the duty of a prince to be liberal, for example, he gradually introduces his own impoverished state and asks for help. In speaking of prudence he brings in the question of annuities and the need to pay them once they are granted. In short, here and in many of his poems, he makes no secret of his poverty, and openly or by inference pleads for help.

If we bear in mind the notorious uncertainty which characterized the Exchequer's payments of annuities we can understand something of Hoccleve's anxiety, and the spur that this gave him to write some of his poems. But this is not all the story. The most interesting reasons for Hoccleve's constant shortness of cash are revealed by his own accounts of his life out of office hours. In his poem, entitled *La male regle de T. Hoccleve*, he looks back on twenty years of eating and drinking extravagantly. 'Excesse at bord hath leyd his knyf with me', he writes, and the sign outside the tavern constantly tempted him to enter. Once there, he has to admit:

> I dar nat telle how that the fresshe repeir
> Of Venus femel lusty children deere,
> That so goodly, so shaply were, and feir,
> And so plesant of port and of maneer,
> And feede cowden al a world with cheere,

And of atyr passyngly wel byseye,
At Poules Heed me maden ofte appeere,
To talke of mirthe, and to disporte and pleye.

Ther was sweet wyn ynow thurgh-out the hous,
And wafres thikke; for this compaignie
That I spak of been somwhat likerous,
Where as they mowe a draght of wyn espie,
Sweete, and in workynge hoot for the maistrie
To warme a stomak with ther-of they dranke.
To suffre hem paie had ben no courtesie:
That charge I tooke to wynne love and thanke.

All he got for this, he says, was a kiss or two, for he was a timid man and dared go no further:

Of loves aart yet touched I no deel;
I cowde nat and eek it was no neede:
Had I a kiss I was content ful weel,
Bettre than I wolde han be with the dede:
Ther-on can I but smal: it is no drede:
When that men speke of it in my presence
For shame I wexe as reed as is the gleede.

gleede: glowing coal.

Furthermore he took care to hold his tongue and to keep out of quarrels. Often in summer, coming from the tavern with his head spinning, he would walk to the Strand Bridge and take a boat on the river where he was well known to the boatmen for his liberality, and was eagerly sought after. In winter, too, he would often go by boat to his office, since the Strand was still unpaved, and the way between there and Westminster deep with mire. The boatmen knew well how to tickle his vanity by calling him Master, thus making him feel a made man for ever, and as a consequence he rewarded them even more freely.

At Westminster Gate where he landed he was equally popular amongst the taverners and cooks, and paid whatever they asked, and was delighted to be thought of by them as 'a verray gentil man'.

Naturally he suffered in the long run. For a while, as he exults, no one in the Privy Seal office was so heavy a drinker and sat up at nights as he did, nor was so loth to rise, although two of his fellows were hot competitors and often lay in bed until nine of the morning. As a result, he reflects, his health is broken and his resources spent. Before he embarked on this riotous life he was reasonably well off. Now he is poor and ill, and goes no more to the tavern. His flatterers of former days scorn and deride him. As he surveys his condition he sees that other than his annuity he has but little. He is afraid to steal and ashamed to beg: already he has borrowed a good deal—in short 'body and purs been at oones seeke'. No wonder that he implores the prince to order his annuity to be paid.

This was in 1406. Six years later he is making a similar request and repeats his regrets for his misguided life. By this time, however, he had married. For over twenty years he had hoped that his services would be rewarded by a benefice, but the king did nothing for him. He tells us of his marriage in these words:

> I gasyd longe firste, and waytid faste
> After some benefice, and whan non cam,
> By proces I me weddid atte laste.
> And, God it wot, it sore me agaste
> To bynde me where I was at my large;
> But done it was: I toke on me that charge.

That was the end of any idea of promotion in the Church. The debauches of his youth were over, and the most he could look forward to now were the meetings of the dining club to which he and other officials belonged, or to occasional feasts such as that given on May Day, 1410, by Sir Henry Somer, chancellor of the Exchequer.

Since as he tells us he had married for love, not for money, he and his wife lived as best they might in their 'smale cote', Hoccleve working by day at the office, and when hard pressed writing a poem in hope of reward. His youthful excesses seem to have damaged his health for a time, and for some five years he suffered from a 'wyld infirmyte' and was out of his mind. He recovered, and with sight impaired and mind enfeebled he struggled on until, after thirty-six years' service, in 1424, he was granted 'such sustenance yearly during his life in the Priory of Southwick, Hants, as Nicholas Mokkinge, late master of St Lawrence in the Poultry, had'.

The king was able to quarter him on the Priory in this manner since, in accordance with medieval practice, he had the right to pension off one of his servants in this way from time to time and the Priory was forced to find suitable accommodation for the corrodian, as he was called, as well as food, amenities and clothing. Unfortunately we do not know the details of Hoccleve's corrody, but in common with many others of the period we may assume that it provided lodging within or close to the precincts of the monastery for Hoccleve and his wife, together with a fixed daily allowance of ale and bread, and a dish of flesh or fish according to the day and season. In addition there were his allowances of wood and candles, yearly robes for himself and his wife and possibly a small grant of money.

Here presumably Hoccleve saw out the remainder of his life in this pleasant Hampshire village, with its undulating country on the edge of the great forest of Bere. Here, under the shadow of the Priory, he could watch the quiet passage of the days while he recalled his memories of the past, his 'skittish youth', his friends, his dining club, his marriage, his 'wyld infirmyte', and perhaps most of all his friendship with the great Chaucer.

When Hoccleve first went to work at the Privy Seal office, Chaucer was a knight of the shire for Kent, and soon after clerk of the works at Westminster Palace and elsewhere, and it may well be that he first met Hoccleve at Westminster. Not only are there many signs of Chaucer's influence throughout Hoccleve's work but he says himself that he was accustomed to receive counsel and advice from Chaucer, and that Chaucer tried to teach him 'but I was dul, and lerned lite or naght'. He learnt enough, however, to recognize genius when he saw it, and the most moving lines he ever wrote are a threnody on 'fadir Chaucer, my dere maistir'.

> But weylaway! so is myn herte wo,
>   That the honour of Englyssh tonge is deed,
>   Of which I wont was han conseil and reed.
>
> O maister deere, and fadir reverent,
>   My maister Chaucer, flour of eloquence,
> Mirour of fructuous entendement,
>   O universal fadir in science,
>   Allas, that thou thyn excellent prudence
>   In thy bed mortel mightist noght byquethe!
>   What eiled deth, allas! why wold he sle the?
>
> She myght han taryed hir vengeance a while
>   Till that some man had egal to the be.
> Nay, lat be that! sche knew wel that this yle
>   May never man forth brynge lyk to the,

And hir office nedes do mot she;
  God bad hir do so, I truste as for the beste;
  O maister, maister, God thi soule reste.

Hoccleve carried his love for Chaucer even further, for in the margin of his poem, *The Regement of Princes*, from which these lines are taken, he set opposite the following verse a portrait of Chaucer in a black hood and gown, with a string of black beads and penner on a red string. The words run:

Al-thogh his lyfe be queynt, the resemblaunce
  Of him hath in me so fressh lyflynesse,
That, to put other men in rémembraunce
  Of his persone, I have heere hys lyknesse
  Do make, to this ende in sothfastnesse,
    That they that have of him lest thought and mynde,
    By this peynture may ageyn him fynde.

queynt: quenched.

When he wrote this Chaucer had been dead about twelve years, while Hoccleve had another twenty-five to live. But his praise of Chaucer was not the extravagant flourish of a disciple. It was only too true that there was no one like Chaucer to succeed him, and Hoccleve felt himself to be alone. For years he had complained of ill-health, so that he may not have been unready to go when the end came about 1437.

The story which Hoccleve has to tell of his life and works, fascinating as it is, still leaves much unsaid that we should like to know concerning the writer's life in the fifteenth century. Naturally in most cases authors say little about themselves, and what they say is common form, as when they lament over their own limited poetical ability, or their general ignorance and lack of understanding. However, these drawbacks did not prevent them from putting pen to paper, and at such times scraps of information concerning themselves, their reasons for writing, and the ends they hoped to achieve emerge, and help us to recreate the literary conditions of the age.

The man of letters who was solely dependent on his pen simply did not exist at this time. It is true that a new class of writers was slowly coming into being—men such as Chaucer or Hoccleve—who had a safe money-making occupation which left them with sufficient leisure to write, but for the most part it was still true to say that the majority of writers were ecclesiastics, writing now and then as a relaxation, or as a part-time hobby, or as a pious duty. Their work presumably pleased themselves, and no doubt they hoped it would please others, and if that pleasure also carried with it a cash reward—so much the better. But their monastery or their rectory assured them of a roof and sustenance while they waited and hoped that their writings would bring them fame.

It is difficult for us to realize how comparatively isolated the medieval writer found himself. He had none of the modern resources of publicity which can easily make a writer's work known wherever that is required. He knew little of what other writers were doing. A visit to London or to one of the large towns of England would have enabled him, by inquiry at the scriveners' shops, to learn what was new and what was in demand. But for the most part he was dependent on the gossip of passing travellers or on the news which circulated in his own countryside. A French or Latin book could well be put into a Northern

English form at the same time that it was being translated in London. Years might pass before anyone knew of the two versions. Only a very few writers had what we should call a national reputation, and most of these appear to have owed their fame to the religious or didactic nature of the subject-matter rather than to the literary skill with which it was handled. Writers were therefore, for the most part, concerned with a local rather than a widespread demand, and they largely depended on the zeal with which their works were praised by individual readers for any circulation they might have. This might take several forms. Sometimes the enthusiasm of one reader caused another to ask a scrivener for a copy of the work; sometimes men had copies made to present to a relative or a friend to mark some special occasion, or to present to one in authority whom he desired to please. At other times an author would be asked not for a copy of an old work, but for a new one. Funds might even be promised for such a labour, while in its turn this new work might provoke another—and so on.

Something of all this may be seen in more detail by looking at the writings of one Osbern Bokenham, an Austin canon of the house of Stoke Clare in south-west Suffolk. We know next to nothing of him: his birthplace has never been exactly determined, and the date of his birth is only inferred to be about '1392' on the strength of a statement in 1443 that he had passed 'ful yerys fyfty'. He had travelled a certain amount, for he mentions both Venice and Montefiascone on the lake of Bolsena, while he also made a pilgrimage to St James of Compostella in Spain. Beyond that we are ignorant of his upbringing and of his life as an Austin canon. His main interest to us arises from a volume of his poems preserved in a single manuscript, now in the British Museum (Arundel 327). It contains thirteen legends of saints and other holy women and runs to over ten thousand lines of verse. The poems are all translations from various Latin sources and are of little or no interest as poetry, and are likely to repel the modern reader by their continuous and long-drawn-out realistic accounts of the sufferings of these holy maidens at the hands of a number of singularly brutal and sadistic oppressors. They merit attention, however, because their author has prefixed to a number of them an account of how they came to be written in which he tells us much about himself and his relation to various people.

It was in response to the request of a friend, one Thomas Burgh, that Bokenham wrote the first of his surviving poems. He tells us that Burgh importuned him to compose a life of St Margaret for whom Burgh had a particular affection. Bokenham asserts that he took time to consider this request, knowing his own poetic 'infirmity', but at last felt that kindness to his friend compelled him to write. As was proper poetic form, he said that he feared the sharp tongues of envious and malicious detractors; and therefore he asks his friend not to divulge his name at present, especially to the members of his friary at Cambridge, where there are many men, subtle and captious of mind, who would quickly see through his incapacity. If later he thought it proper to give the work a wider circulation, Bokenham asks him to say that it was written by a friend, living near Burgh's birthplace, who used to sell horses at fairs! In this way, says Bokenham, he will escape suspicion. Having thus protected his anonymity, Bokenham commenced to write on 7 September

1443, and fourteen days later had composed 920 lines of rhyming couplets. At this point, feeling the strain of composition, he took a few days off, before going on to the second part of the poem which ran to another 480 lines. A rest, he says, is necessary, for both his pen and himself are worn out. His wits are failing, and so are his eyes, while his hand begins to tremble. As for his pen, it has been made to go over the page so many times that it no longer runs easily, and thus makes many a blot. So he craves for a rest—but only a short one, and promises to start again, some ten days hence, after Michaelmas Day.

Bokenham had evidently no great ambition to be known as a poet if we may believe what he says, and certainly if this was his first poetical work in English (and we know of no other) he was late in the field, since he was fifty at the time, and probably died at the age of fifty-four. His poetical gifts were known, however, in his neighbourhood, and the next poem in the volume was written at the request of Katherine Denston. Now the Denston family lived only eight miles from Bokenham's friary, and had evidently importuned him to write the life of St Anne, and despite age and doubts as to his ability he finally consented. Before beginning the poem proper, however, he indulges in a hundred lines of apologetics: he lacks skill and eloquence; his language is but ordinary, for unlike Chaucer, Gower and Lydgate, he has never drunk of the streams of Helicon or been taught by Orpheus. Besides, 'death hath at my gate, drawn up his cart to carry me hence', and it would be better for him to amend his life and search his conscience rather than to indulge in worldly matters. We need not take all this too seriously: most poets protested at length of their inferiority and unwillingness to write—but write they do, and generally at no small length.

So Bokenham at last comes to the life of St Anne the mother of the Blessed Virgin. He tells of the miraculous birth of 'Maid Mary', and rapidly brings his poem to a close, saying that he has already told of St Anne's three daughters in Latin verses. They were all called Mary, but whether St Anne had one husband or three, Bokenham does not know. He concludes with a prayer to the Saint, asking a blessing on John and Katherine Denston, and on their daughter Anne, and beseeching her to intercede that the Denstons may be given a son.

The mention of this family at the beginning and end of his poem by Bokenham is significant. Here was a well-to-do, influential family whose patronage and support were of sufficient importance for Bokenham to bring their names in this way into his poem. He must have known that whenever the poem was read it was but a step for the curious to learn that the author was a canon of a nearby friary. So Bokenham's reputation spread. If we were in any doubt of this, we have only to turn to the prologue to his life of St Mary Magdalene. On Twelfth Night, 1445, Bokenham tells us that he was in the presence of the countess of Eu, wife of Henry Bouchier, sometime earl of Essex. Her four sons were there, each of them clad in brightly coloured garments, and while they were dancing and revelling about the chamber, the countess talked to Bokenham of the many legends which by this time he had put into English, and particularly of one recently begun at the request of the countess of Oxford. She went on to say that she had for long cherished a particular affection for St Mary Magdalene, and desired Bokenham to write an English life of the Saint. This at first he hesitated (he tells us) to perform, but after thinking it over agreed to do so, provided he might first make a pilgrimage to Compostella which he had promised to undertake, since this was a 'year of grace' at the shrine, a time when fuller remission and absolution from sin was available than in ordinary years. To this the lady Bouchier agreed, and immediately on his return from Compostella, Bokenham (with his customary excuses) began to write a life of the saint.

Much about this time Bokenham also composed a life of St Katherine for two ladies—Katherine Denston, of whom we have heard before, and Katherine Howard, wife of John Howard, of Stoke Neyland, who lived only sixteen miles from Stoke Clare. Bokenham says that John Capgrave had but recently written a life of the saint, but since that work is hard to come by, he will tell of her sufferings as best he can for the ghostly consolation of the two ladies. He must have worked at a good pace, for in five days he had written no less than 1000 lines of rhyming couplets! We cannot expect that in such circumstances work of any quality will be produced, and Bokenham does not disappoint our expectations. The ladies, no doubt, were duly edified, and still more important, were duly gratified to find their names enshrined in a poem written by the famous local poet. Capgrave and his work were but names to them: years might elapse before they were able to get a copy of his poem, but here, a few days after the asking, they had their poem, and let us hope that Bokenham had his reward, both in cash and in reputation.

Three more similar works were written by Bokenham to please influential neighbours. The legend of St Dorothy was composed for John Hunt and his wife Isobel, while that of St Agatha was meant for her namesake, Agatha Flegge. Finally, the legend of St Elizabeth was made for Elizabeth de Vere, countess of Oxford, to whom, says Bokenham, he neither can, will, nor may say no, so much is he indebted to her kindness.

So we come to an end of the known writings of Bokenham, who died shortly after these poems were written. He serves as an interesting example of the way some poetry of the period came into being, and it will be noted that it is only the chance that his various verses were collected into one volume that has preserved them for us. The individual poems, written and given to the several families concerned, have all long since disappeared. How many other poems, written in various parts of fifteenth-century England have gone the same way we shall never know.

MARGARET PASTON

AT the time when Sir John Fastolf returned to England and to his Norfolk home, there was growing up in another part of the county a young girl whose letters as a married woman were to become famous in later centuries. Margaret Mauteby was the daughter of a Norfolk landowner of some importance—indeed of sufficient importance for the wealthy and distinguished judge, William Paston, of the Bench of Common Pleas, to look favourably on her family when he was seeking a bride for his son and heir, John Paston. The Pastons at this time were a rising family: William Paston had prospered in the law, and by a judicious marriage, and by the steady buying of manors, had become a considerable landowner. The Mautebys, on their side, were people of good family and wealth, and a union between the two houses had much to commend it from a worldly point of view—and such a point of view was nine-tenths of the matter in fifteenth-century matchmaking.

The story begins soon after Easter, about the year 1440. A letter from Agnes Paston to her husband in London, where he was occupied on the Bench, told him of the first appearance of Margaret at their house. The judge had arranged for such a meeting before he left Norfolk, and Agnes delightedly writes:

Blessed be God I send you good tidings of the coming and bringing home of the young gentlewoman that you know of from Reedham this same night.... And as for the first acquaintance between John Paston and the said gentlewoman, she made him gentle cheer in gentle wise, and said he was verily your son. And so I hope there shall need no great treaty between them.

No difficulties appear to have arisen: the desires of their parents were an overwhelming factor, and neither John nor Margaret proved unwilling, and thus began a marriage destined to last for twenty-five years, during which time Margaret's devotion to her husband and wholehearted service to his interests seem never to have flagged. In a remarkable series of letters written to him (and after his death to his sons), Margaret portrays for us what it meant to be the wife of a property-owner in the middle years of the fifteenth century, and what burdens and responsibilities she carried, both as a mother and as a housewife.

We would give much for an account of the early days of such a marriage as this. How long did it take for these victims of a *mariage de convenance* to get used to one another? When and how did this relation turn into one of deep affection? How soon was Margaret shouldering the day-to-day burdens of the estate? To these and other questions we can give no answer, save to note that John was still a student at Cambridge at the time of the marriage, and it appears that Margaret was left at home with her mother-in-law while he returned to his studies at Peterhouse. From there he went to London to the Inner Temple and Margaret's letter to him, written some three years after their marriage, shows how far she had fallen in love with him during that time. John was sick in London,

and Margaret pours out her heart to him more unreservedly than ever again, when she writes:

Right worshipful husband, I recommend me unto you, desiring to hear of your welfare, thanking God of your amending of the great disease that you have had. And I thank you for the letter that you sent me, for by my troth, my mother [i.e. Agnes] and I were nought in heart's ease from the time that we knew of your sickness till we knew truly of your amending. My mother promised another image of wax to the weight of you to Our Lady of Walsingham, and she sent four nobles [26*s.* 8*d.*] to the Friars at Norwich to pray for you, and I have promised to go on pilgrimage to Walsingham and to Saint Leonard's [Priory Norwich] for you. By my troth, I had never so heavy a season as I had from the time that I knew of your sickness till I knew of your amending, and yet my heart is in no great ease, nor shall be until I know that ye be very well...I pray you heartily that [ye] will vouchsafe to send me a letter as hastily as ye may, if writing be no dis-ease to you, and that ye will vouchsafe to send me word how your sore doeth. If I might have had my will I should have seen you ere this time. I would ye were at home, if it were to your ease, and your sore might be as well looked to here as it is there [where] you are now, rather than a gown [even] though it were of scarlet. I pray you if your sore be whole, and so that ye may endure to ride, when my father comes to London that ye will ask leave and come home when the horse shall be sent home again, for I hope you should be kept as tenderly here as ye be in London. I may no leisure have to write half a quarter as much as I should say to you if I might speak with you. I shall send you another letter as hastily as I may. Almighty God have you in his keeping and send you health....My mother greets you well, and sends you God's blessing and hers; and she prayeth you, and I pray you also, that ye be well dieted of meat and drink, for that is the greatest help that ye may have now to your health ward.

So began this *mariage de convenance*, and while Margaret is unusually explicit here, from time to time in the next twenty years a phrase creeps in among the mass of business and domestic detail which she reports to her husband which shows how deeply her affections were engaged. After some twenty years of married life she could say: 'I thank you heartily for your letter, for it was to me a great comfort to hear from you', and she constantly reminds him that she can never have ease until he writes, and that he cannot write too often. She urges him: 'Be not strange of writing letters to me betwixt this and [the time] that you come home. If I might, I would have one every day from you.' John Paston appears to have been of a somewhat reserved disposition: for him she is 'my own dear sovereign lady', and her illness causes him to write: 'John Hobbs tells me that you are sickly, which melikes not to hear. Praying you heartily that you take what may do you ease and spare not: and in anywise take no thought nor too much labour for these matters [of business] nor set it not so to your heart that you fare the worse for it.' Farther than that he cannot go; but this was evidently enough, since we must remember that John's position as head of the family placed him something apart, not only from his children, but from his wife. Her letters begin: 'Right worshipful husband, I recommend me unto you', and this is more than a formal address: it is a recognition of a relationship which had centuries of use behind it. His children, again, show even more clearly the unique position of the father in the medieval household, and when they write, they begin with some such phrase as: 'Most reverent and worshipful father, I recommend me heartily, and submit me lowly to your good fatherhood, beseeching you for charity of your daily blessing.'

In her letter quoted above, when John lay sick in

London, Margaret added a postscript: 'Your son fareth well, blessed be God', thus referring to her first born, afterwards to become Sir John Paston. There were at least six children, and from time to time we learn something of them and of their affairs. In conformity with medieval ideas they played a distinctly inferior role. The notion that children had any natural rights was almost impossible to a medieval mind. Agnes Paston tells a schoolmaster to 'truly belash' her son Clement if he has not done well, for 'so did his last master...the best he ever had at Cambridge...for I would rather he were fairly buried than lost for lack of correction'. She practised what she preached, for when her daughter Elizabeth refused to agree to their mother's plan to marry her to 'a battered old widower', Agnes kept her for weeks in solitary confinement, and her cousin said that for three months she had 'for the most part been beaten once in the week or twice, sometimes twice in a day, and her head broken in two or three places'.

Margaret was not as harsh as this, but her children were kept severely in their place, and any sign of rebellion was mercilessly stamped out, as her eldest son found when he offended his father on some matter. Although he was of age, he was promptly exiled to a distant family manor and there left to cool his temper, from whence he wrote in due time:

May it please your fatherhood to remember and consider the pain and heaviness that it has been to me since your departing out of this country. I am here abiding till the time that by report, my demeaning may be to your pleasing. Wherefore I beseech you of your fatherly pity to tender the more kindly this simple writing, as I shall out of doubt hereafter do that which shall please you, to the uttermost of my power and labour. And if there be any service that I may do, if it please you to command me, and if I may understand it, I will be as glad to do it as anything on earth, if it were anything that might be to your pleasing.

Even this did not placate his father, and a further period of exile, and his mother's entreaty: 'I beseech you heartily that you vouchsafe to be his good father, for I hope he is chastised, and will be worthier here after', were necessary before his father would relent.

John did not fulfil his mother's hopes, and again we find her pleading for him: 'For God's sake Sir, have pity on him', but when at length this man of twenty-five is allowed to return, Margaret hastens to assure her husband that she will not tolerate any behaviour on her son's part that is not strictly proper: 'I pray you think not of me that I will support him or favour him in any lewdness [bad behaviour], for I will not. As I find him hereafter, so will I let you have knowledge.' Margaret was certainly less harsh than her husband, but even so, she expected much of her children, and their life at home was far from happy.

Home, indeed, was not a place where most children of well-to-do families were allowed to stay *sine die*. Whenever possible a place was found for them in the entourage of a rich or neighbouring family. If parents could get children domiciled in the house of a great lord, or of some influential person, their chances of advancement or of a good marriage were greatly enhanced. Paston's eldest son, therefore, was attached to the king's court for a while, and his second son was placed in the household of the young duke of Norfolk. As for the girls, Margaret went to work with great circumspection, for she had no intention of letting them live with nobodies. Her directions on this point are clear and explicit, so that she writes to her son:

> As for your sister being with my Lady, if your father will agree thereto, I hold me right well pleased. For I would be right glad that she should do her service before any other,—if she could do what should please my Lady's good grace. Wherefore I would that you should speak to your father thereof,... for I would be right glad if she might be preferred by marriage, or by service, so that it be to her worship and profit.

Marriage, service, worship, profit—it was in these terms that a young girl's life was thought of, so that a position in the household of 'my Lady of Oxford, or with my Lady of Bedford, or in some other worshipful place', was mentioned by Margaret as a desirable home for her daughter, for there she would make friends with influential people, and might even attract the attention of an eligible husband. Apart from these considerations, Margaret does not seem to have had much affection for her daughters, and says frankly at one point: 'we be either of us weary of the other'; and at another, a complaint of one of the girls is rebuffed with the remark that 'she must use herself to work readily, as other gentlewomen do, and somewhat to help herself'. Whether at home or away, life for these young people was harsh, and the Venetian envoy to England about 1500 was horrified by the presence of these youngsters in other people's houses, and writes to his master:

> The want of affection in the English is strongly manifested towards their children: for after having kept them at home till they arrive at the age of 7 or 9 years at the utmost, they put them out, both males and females, to hard service in the

houses of others...and few are born who are exempted from this fate, for everyone however rich he may be, sends away his children into the houses of others, while he, in return, receives those of strangers into his own.

The day came, however, when the children could no longer be boarded out, and the search for a suitable marriage was begun. With several boys and girls all to be considered Margaret was for some years seldom without worries attendant on the progress of this or that possibility of a good match. Her eldest son never married, although he was known as 'the best chooser of a gentlewoman', and was a great favourite of the ladies. At one time he had an affair that lasted nine years, but he was usually much busier on the matrimonial ventures of other members of the family than on his own. His brother John on the other hand must have caused his mother much anxiety, for he was of a full-blooded amorous disposition which forced him to write to his brother to get him 'a wife somewhere, for "melius est enim nubere quam uri"'. We may sympathize with Margaret as we read of the failure of one match after another—with Lady Boleyn's daughter, or Katherine Dudley, or Elizabeth Bouchier. Merchants' daughters, a 'thrifty old draff-wyff', a Blackfriar's widow, or anyone with a suitable fortune were eagerly considered, but for one reason or another abandoned. Then he heard of a Norfolk lady, Margery Brews by name, who was much praised by a friend, and before long we find him offering her his 'poor heart that sometime was at my rule, which is now at yours'. He really was in earnest this time, and with her mother's aid he worked to win this girl as he had never done before. The battle was not easy, for his brother and his mother were naturally doubtful as to his sincerity, while Sir Thomas Brews was even more uncertain of his suitability as a match for his daughter. Fortunately for John, Margery was overwhelmingly in love with him and wrote:

> My mother hath laboured the matter to my father full diligently, but she can get no more [money] than ye know of ...for the which, God knoweth, I am full sorry. But if ye love me, as I trust verily that ye do...ye will not leave me therefore, for if ye had not half the livelode that ye have, for to do the greatest labour that any woman alive might, I would not forsake you.

This and other letters of hers testify to her ardour, while John himself won over his mother, and at last overcame the difficulties raised by Sir Thomas, and brought her home as his bride.

His sister Margery also caused the family much trouble over her marriage. Her brother received a number of unsuitable offers for her hand, and her mother had taken her to the rood at the north door of St Paul's and also to St Saviour's Abbey, Bermondsey, 'to pray to them that she may have a good husband'. For several years after this she remained unmarried, but her affections were not unengaged, for she had fallen in love and given binding pledges to Richard Calle the family bailiff. Now the formal plighting of troth between two people at that time was absolutely binding. No witnesses were required and no ceremony other than the actual plighting of the two lovers. The Church discouraged these secret engagements, but could not untie them. This the Pastons knew as well as did Calle, and part of the tremendous scenes that took place when the betrothal was announced by Margery were no doubt due to the undoubted fact that what was done could not be undone. Her brothers protested, her mother stormed, but the lovers stood firm. 'This is a painful life we lead', wrote Calle, 'I suppose they think we be not betrothed together, and if they do I marvel, for then they are not well advised, remembering the plainness that I broke [the matter] to my mistress at the beginning, and I suppose by you as well.' Of course Margaret knew, and when nothing else would do she took the matter to the bishop of Norwich, who called Margery and Calle before him, made her repeat the words she had used in binding herself to Calle so that he might see if they were binding and sufficient, and found himself unable to find any flaw in them. Margaret, however, remained adamant and when the girl returned home refused her admission, so that she had to seek refuge in a nearby nunnery, until such time as the lovers could be married. Her mother's attitude was expressed in a letter to her son: 'I pray you...that ye take it not pensively, for I know well it goeth right near your heart, and so it doth to mine and others. But remember you, and so do I that we have lost of her but a worthless person...for if he [Calle] were dead at this hour, she should never be at my heart as she was.' So matters had to be left, and the lovers were married shortly after; and since Margaret left the sum of £20 when she died to Margery's eldest child, we may believe that the breach between mother and daughter was ultimately healed.

There was work enough to occupy Margaret besides her husband and children. John Paston was a man of some importance in the county, and his home reflected this in its size and organization. Much of the work of running such a house fell on Margaret, for the medieval wife was essentially a housewife. Much of her time, therefore, was devoted to the very considerable task of providing meat and drink in sufficient quantity to meet the needs of a household, constantly fluctuating in number, and liable at short notice to entertain guests of some importance. To this end it was necessary for her to look well ahead. A lack of forethought on her part in autumn might very well mean a lack of food several months hence. The medieval housewife had to store, and preserve, and spin, in order to have ever ready to hand the means of life. No family could sit down to a single meal without eating and drinking things either made in the house, or prepared for the table by the good wife and her servants. The brewhouse and the bakehouse, the dairy and the kitchens all needed her constant attention. To this end we see her laying in her Lenten supply of fish, or her autumn beef for salting down for the winter months. She tells of going into Norwich to buy such things as she needed for the winter, or of asking her husband to send sugar or treacle. Medieval cookery made great play with spices, and Paston or his sons is asked from time to time to buy pepper, cloves, mace, ginger, cinnamon, almonds, rice and other foreign commodities. Dates and oranges were frequently asked for, and were greatly desired by women approaching confinement, while London prices were carefully scrutinized and compared with those of Norwich before Margaret placed her order. Much of what she required was produced on the family manors; so that supplies of grain and of foodstuffs were constantly arriving; the hedges and wastes were flushed for birds; rabbits and hares were trapped and the dovecote and poultry-yard frequently raided to produce the many foodstuffs that were necessary to keep even an ordinary squire's table decently and adequately furnished.

From the household book of another family comparable with the Pastons we can see in exact terms what a burden was placed on the housewife. A typical entry runs:

> Victuals expended throughout the month [August, 1413]. Wheat baked, 8 quarters 4 bushels; wine [blank]; barley and drage malt brewed, 18 quarters; beef, 2 carcasses, 3 quarters; pork, 5 pigs and 1 quarter; 1 young pig; 22 carcasses of mutton; 2 lambs; 1 capon; 333 pigeons; 1 heron; 460 white herrings; 18 salt fish; 6 stockfish.

The reason for such a mass of food is given when we turn to see the numbers to be catered for daily. To take the first of August as an example: on this day the lady entertained a friend, and sat down with eight of her household to all meals, and in addition the harvest-reeve and sixteen workers came to the manor hall for their midday repast. As a result the pantry had to provide some sixty loaves, and an unspecified amount of ale, while the kitchen used a quarter-side of beef, another of bacon, one joint of mutton and twelve pigeons. Each day throughout the month similar demands were made upon the supplies, and an inspection of the book over a twelvemonth reveals that many members of the families of the neighbourhood paid visits from time to time, as well as callers on business or folk seeking aid or advice. All of these had to be entertained in a style befitting the position held by the family in the county; and in the case of the Pastons it was on Margaret's shoulders in the main that the burden fell.

Furthermore, there was much to be done to provide

clothing for the needs of a growing family. Ready-made garments were unknown, so that the household was constantly occupied in making clothes of all kinds, and in keeping up the stock of household linen. To this end Margaret bought material, usually in Norwich, but would at times write to her husband in London asking him to

> buy some frieze to make your child's gowns. You shall have best cheap and best choice of Hay's wife as it is told me. And that you will buy a yard of broad-cloth of black for a hood for me at 3*s*. 8*d*. or 4*s*. a yard, for there is neither good cloth or good frieze in this town [Norwich]. As for the child's gowns if I have [the stuff] I will get them made.

Margaret frequently asked her husband or her sons in London to enquire of the price and quality of various materials, and things such as hats, or girdles or hose. She left little to chance, or to the vagaries of masculine taste, but instructed the unfortunate man to

> buy me three yards of purple schamlet, price to the yard 4*s*.; a bonnet of deep murrey, price 2*s*. 4*d*.; a hose-cloth of yellow-carsey of an ell, I trow it will cost 2*s*.; a girdle of plunket ribbon, price 6*d*.; four laces of silk, two of one colour and two of another, price 8*d*.; 3 dozen points with red and yellow, price 6*d*.; three pairs of pattens....I was wont to pay but 2½*d*. for a pair, but I pray you let them not be left behind though I pay more. They must be low pattens; let them be long enough and broad upon the heel.

All these things had to be at hand and ready for use when required, while in addition Margaret had the overseeing, repair and replenishment of the great variety of household fabrics and fittings that were an essential part of a gentleman's establishment. When the duke of Suffolk raided the Paston's manor of Hellesdon he took away (*inter alia*) from the bed-chambers, two feather beds and two bolsters; four mattresses and four bolsters: two canopies with their curtains of blue buckram and white linen cloth; pillows, coverlets of divers colours; sheets, blankets, etc. Even when no such losses were sustained the upkeep and replacement from time to time of 'sore-worn' pieces must have kept Margaret busy, the more so when we remember that these were but part of the furnishings of two rooms.

It might well be thought that Margaret had plenty to occupy her in attending to these many duties, and so she had; yet at the same time her attention and energies were constantly devoted to other matters. John Paston was frequently absent in London for long periods, for the task of fighting in the law-courts to protect himself against the attacks of those striving to despoil him of parts of his property necessitated his constant presence and vigilance there. This left Margaret in charge of his business affairs in Norfolk, and from the start she showed remarkable ability as a shrewd and careful administrator. She received her husband's instructions, carried them out, reported action taken and warned him of his enemies' moves with great efficiency, and at the same time was not slow in taking things into her own hands when necessary. So she negotiated with farmers, threatened lawsuits and made distraints; endeavoured to placate opponents and angry tenants; sent agents to buy and sell, to hold courts, to entreat with the justices and great lords—in short there was little that her husband could do that she did not attempt. Her letters give a full account of her activities. Thus she tells her husband in one of them that she encloses a deed wanted to prove a title, and promises more if they are found; warns him of a possible attempt to seize one of his manors; asks for instructions concerning the sale of last year's malt which may rapidly deteriorate in the hot weather; advises him not to let one of his marshes this year, so that his poor tenants may gather rushes to repair their houses. She advises him to let the poorest of them have the windfall wood for a similar purpose, and tells him of her efforts to let another marsh. In her next letter she says that she has seen and put courage into the tenants at Drayton who were being threatened by the duke of Suffolk, 'and they will be glad to have their old master, ...except one or two that be false shrews'. Next week, she says, she will go to another of his manors and try to raise some money and hold a manor court. His instructions about selling the barley and malt shall be carried out, and certain documents she will seal up in a sack and put away secretly. The horse of a tenant has unjustly been seized, but Margaret says that if she cannot get it, it will be the worse for the captor! This, and half a dozen other things in the letter all go to testify to the energy and capability of this woman.

In addition courage was required of her, for she lived in a turbulent age, when naked force was constantly employed, and men were often afraid to defy their oppressors. Margaret tells her husband that no one would go to plead with the visiting justices at Norwich on his behalf, and so she had to go herself, and this courage never forsook her, although at times she was wellnigh worn out. Three times she saw her home taken from her by armed gangs of men who attacked the houses in overwhelming force, and ejected Margaret and her servants, pulling down timbers and doors and robbing the tenants' houses. These things were bad enough, but they were only the culmination of periods of fear when the enemies of the Pastons were in the ascendant, and when Margaret and her servants went abroad in some danger. From time to time her letters betray something of the strain she was under, but for the main part she accepted it as part of the day's work, and was not above using a measure of force herself if the opportunity served. The treatment Margaret had to endure while acting on her husband's behalf is set out in Paston's petition to the king in which he relates how on

> the 18th day of January last past, lord Moleyns sent to the said mansion [of Gresham] a riotous people to the number of a thousand persons...arrayed in manner of war, with cuirasses, coats of mail, steel helmets, glaives, bows, arrows, large shields, guns, pans with fire, long cromes [hooks] to draw down houses, ladders and picks with which they mined down the walls, and long trees with which they broke up gates and doors, and so came into the said mansion, the wife of your beseecher at that time being therin, and twelve persons with her—the which persons they drove out of the mansion, and mined down the walls of the chamber wherin the wife of your beseecher was, and bare her out at the gates, and cut asunder the posts of the houses, and let them fall, and broke up all the chambers and coffers in the mansion, and rifled...and bare away stuff, array and money...to the value of £200.

On another occasion it was the duke of Suffolk who was the aggressor, and Margaret had to protect her husband's claim to the manor of Drayton by a series of vigorous actions. After preliminary skirmishes on either side, Margaret seized some seventy-seven head of cattle, saying that she would hold them until rents were paid to her and not to the duke. The duke's agent told the tenants not to pay, protested with Margaret, and finally got a writ from the sheriff of Norfolk, which Margaret dared not disobey, and so the beasts were surrendered. Throughout the summer of 1465 this duel went on, both sides using force and invoking the law as opportunity served. Margaret was almost worn out, and appeals to her husband in London:

> Right worshipful husband, I recommend me to you, praying you heartily that you will seek means that your servants may be in peace, for they be daily in fear of their lives.... It were well done that you should speak with the Justices ere they come here. If you will that I complain to them, or to any other, if God fortune me life and health, I will do as you advise, for in good faith.... what with sickness and trouble that I have had, I am brought right low and weak, but to my power I will do as I can or may in your matters.

Her husband was of little help, for shortly after he was thrown into the Fleet prison. Margaret determined to hold a manor court at Drayton—the most significant sign of ownership possible—but no one save her domestic chaplain, Thomas Bond, was willing to run the risk of trying to preside. A force of sixty or seventy men awaited Bond at the court, arrested him 'and bound his arms behind him with whipcord like a thief'. Margaret at once sought an audience with the justices, laid the whole matter before them and so convincingly set out her case, that they freed Bond at once and severely censured the duke's officers. Margaret was so delighted that, in her excitement when writing to her husband, she described the scene before the judges twice over!

Paston's death in 1466 at once threw a mass of work on Margaret and her helpers, for preparations had to be made for the burial. The body was brought from

London and lay at St Peter's, Hungate, in Norwich, where a solemn dirge was sung by friars of the four Orders, and a gathering of thirty-eight priests, thirty-four boys in surplices, and twenty-six clerks sang and prayed for the dead man's soul. Not only these, but the prioress of Carrow, followed by her maid, as well as twenty-three sisters from Norman's Hospital, attended this service. Four torch-bearers stood about the corpse, while the bells of St Peter's and of St Stephen's churches tolled for the dead. After this, the body was carried to Bromholm Priory, and a further great ceremony was held. The details of the preparations made for this service and for the reception and entertaining of the many folk who were present must have thrown a great burden on Margaret. These are the lists showing the varied and numerous stores of food which were ordered, as well as details concerning the arrangements. On the day that Paston was buried at Bromholm, fourteen ringers were employed to toll for him, twenty-four servitors were hired at fourpence a day to wait on the guests, and seventy other servitors at threepence. Eighteen barrels of beer, and a large quantity of malt were laid on, and a runlet of red wine was at hand to serve the needs of the quality.

Once this was over Margaret settled down to her new life and it cannot have been an easy one. Sir John was much in London, but unlike his father was more interested in the life of a man of fashion than that of a man of affairs. 'We beat the bushes and have the loss and the disworship, and other men have the birds', wrote his mother, urging him to take more vigorous action in various matters, but his heart was not really in the immense labour which was necessary if all the Paston lands were to be kept safely within the family. He had his mistress, his beloved books and his social life in London to divert him, even while his mother and his brother John were at their wits' end how to stop their enemies from dislodging them from one piece of property or another. Instead of fighting his enemies in the law-courts he indulged in such pleasures as betting or taking part in tournaments. Speaking of one of the latter he writes to his brother: 'My hand was hurt at the tourney at Eltham upon Wednesday last. I would that you had been there and seen it, for it was the goodliest sight that was seen in England this forty years.' John, troubled by a host of worries in Norfolk which were rightly his brother's lot, replies drily: 'whereas it pleaseth you to wish me to Eltham, at the tourney for the good sight that was there, by truth I had rather see you once in Caister Hall than to see as many King's tourneys as might be between Eltham and London.'

For the rest of her life Margaret was constantly engaged in urging on her sons or in taking action herself. At her right hand was the family domestic chaplain, James Gloys, who came into the service of the Pastons about 1448 and was with them continuously until his death in 1473. Early in his stay with them he had won the confidence of Margaret and this in time gave him so secure a position that he was able to treat the younger members of the family with scant respect. The first time he is mentioned is in terms of dislike by Edmund, and it seems clear that Gloys had been influencing Margaret, since Edmund bursts out angrily: 'Unless among us we give not him a lift, I pray God that we never thrive.' The passage of years seems only to have increased his hold on Margaret, and her house must often have been an uncomfortable place for those who would not bow to his will. As late as 1472, John speaks of him as 'the proud, peevish and evil disposed priest to us all', and goes on later to write: 'Many quarrels are picked to get my brother Edmund and me out of her house. We go not to bed unchided. All that we do is ill done, and all that [Gloys] and Pecock do, is well done....We fell out before my mother with "Thou proud priest", and "Thou proud squire", my mother taking his part.' On another occasion John writes: 'Gloys is always chopping at me when my mother is present, with such words as he thinks anger me, and also cause my mother to be displeased with me...and when he has most unfitting words to me, I smile a little and tell him it is good hearing of these old tales.'

No doubt Margaret's children disliked the position held by Gloys, but it must be admitted that he had become invaluable to his mistress. He was more like an estate overseer or head bailiff than a chaplain, and had a very extensive knowledge of the family's affairs. Moreover, he could do things that Margaret could not attempt in her own person. Thus he makes distraints, attempts to arrest a man despite much interference, and failing in this, lays an ambush for him: 'I lay in wait upon him on the heath, as he should have come homewards, and if I might have met with him I should have had Betts from him: but he had laid such watch that he had espied us before he came fully at us...and he took his horse with his spurs and rode... as fast as he might ride.' Besides all this he got Paston's writs duly attested after considerable trouble; had interviewed (and probably bribed) many men who were to serve on a jury to decide a case between the Pastons and a neighbour, made arrangements for the letting of lands—in short was the right-hand man of Margaret and of all the family—a position recognized by them, however much they complained at times.

As her life drew to a close on 4 February 1482, Margaret 'whole of spirit and mind, with perfect consideration and good deliberation', made her testament and last will, and a study of this enables us to learn much that her letters only partly reveal. Outstanding, of course, is her complete adherence to the faith of her fathers, and her desire to lie with them in the aisle of the family church at Mauteby where she was born. She directs that the aisle shall be heightened, the windows glazed and the roof covered with lead and that twenty shillings shall be given to the high altar. Her grave is to be marked by a stone, bearing the arms of her husband's family and her own, and under the Mauteby arms the words 'In God is my trust'.

At her funeral twelve poor men of her tenantry, clad in white gowns and hoods, were to stand about the bier holding torches, while six candles, each weighing four pounds, burned about the hearse. For seven years following her death a large wax candle was to stand on her grave every Sunday and Holy Day while divine service was said; and, on the anniversary of her death for twelve years following, a service should be held at Mauteby for her and her forebears. Rewards were left for all taking part in these ceremonies and for a special service to be held at St Michael's, Coslany in Norwich for the repose of her soul. In addition a mass-priest was to be appointed, who for seven years would say mass for her and her husband, and for their ancestors, while two large service books costing the considerable sum of £5. 6*s*. 8*d*. were to be placed in the church 'to the worship of God, as long as they may endure'. Many other churches standing on her family manors were helped by gifts of vestments, while many religious foundations received varying sums of money, her parish church of St Peter's, Hungate, Norwich, being left £20 for the augmentation of the parson's salary. So we might go on: item after item in the will testifying to Margaret's devotion to Holy Church. Charitable gifts to persons were not forgotten. All who participated in the services held at her burial were rewarded, according to their degree, while the poor on her manors and the lepers of Norwich and Yarmouth were specially remembered.

Once she had made these dispositions Margaret turned to more worldly matters, and one by one her children and their families are remembered. Her eldest son died unmarried, but Margaret nevertheless left to his bastard daughter the sum of ten marks when she reached the age of twenty. Her second son John was given gold and silver cups and goblets and his wife a mass-book, all her altar-cloths, and a silver pix, while their son and daughter were each to receive one hundred marks when they came of age. Since John had inherited the family properties that was enough: it was on her other children that Margaret bestowed most of her personal possessions. We see the Mauteby best feather-bed with its tapestry, canopy and curtains, as well as blankets, a pair of finest sheets and other stuffs going to her daughter-in-law Anne, as well as a garnish (set) of pewter vessels, basins, ewers, candle-sticks, etc. She also was left the wall-hangings in the parlour at Mauteby, two valuable cups, twelve silver spoons and a blue enamelled powder box, as well as other things. So one by one the old lady went through the list of her relatives and friends leaving to one a girdle, to another a set of beads of chalcedony, to another a gown furred with black. All her servants who were in her employ at the time of her death were to be kept for six months, and then on discharge to be given an additional quarter's wages. When all her wishes had been fulfilled the residue of her estate was to be at the disposition of her executors to spend on 'other deeds of mercy for my soul, my ancestors' souls, and all Christian souls, to the most pleasure of God, and profit to my soul'.

Little remained to do, but evidently about this time when John and his wife Margery were staying with her, Margaret took an opportunity to entreat Margery to persuade her husband to carry out his mother's bequests, which brought from him the forthright declaration: 'Mother...there needeth no ambassadors nor means betwixt you and me: for there is neither wife nor other friend shall make me do that your commandments shall make me to do, if I may have knowledge of it; and if I have no knowledge of it, in good faith I am excusable, both to God and you.' He goes on to give some interesting details of the trouble he had to get her to make a will, and to set down exactly 'what you would have done for yourself, and to your children and servants'. He reminds her that at the making of her will, and in all the discussions about it, he did nothing to go against her wishes, but offered to be bound to perform them exactly. 'And thus have I [done], and ever will be ready unto, while I live, on my faith, and never thought otherwise, so God be my help.'

Let us hope that these assurances satisfied her. The end came soon after on 4 November 1484, and on 18 December, her will was proved. It was nearly twenty years since her husband had died, and forty-four since the day as a young girl she had first entered the Paston household. Yet perhaps it was her birthplace of Mauteby that had her heart. Despite the Paston's name and standing in the county, it was to Mauteby that her remains were carried, and there in the aisle of Mauteby Church her monument bore the proud words: 'Here lieth Margaret Paston, late the wife of John Paston, daughter and heir of John Mauteby, Squire...on whose soul God have mercy.'

MARGERY KEMPE

AMONG the many little books—scarcely more than pamphlets—printed by Wynkyn de Worde in his efforts to provide reading matter for the growing literate public of his day, was a small eight-page quarto pamphlet—'A short treatise of contemplation taught by Our Lord, Jesu Christ, taken out of the book of Margery Kempe of Lynn'. Wynkyn de Worde may have printed some five hundred copies of this work, but in the course of centuries all of these save one seem to have perished, and from a study of the only known copy in the University Library, Cambridge, it was long thought that the work was a condensed version of a book of devotions, similar to that of other religious writers of the time, such as Hilton's *Scale of Perfection*, or the *Revelations* of Dame Juliana of Norwich. In 1934, however, Miss Hope Emily Allen, well known for her work on Robert Rolle and other mystics, announced her identification of a manuscript in the library of Colonel Butler-Bowdon of Pleasington Old Hall, Lancashire, as the autobiography of Margery Kempe, from which Wynkyn de Worde had extracted a mere handful of sentences.

Here then we have what Professor R. W. Chambers called 'our first biography in English'—a work in which the life, thoughts and experiences of a religious enthusiast are set out in detail. A generation earlier Geoffrey Chaucer had set down the thoughts and experiences of a sensual woman of the bourgeoisie in his portrait of the Wife of Bath. In her autobiography Margery Kempe, with a similar bourgeois background, unfolds for us the anxieties and experiences of a religious woman whose life was dedicated to the service of God. No English writer, hitherto, had committed to writing so intimate, revealing and human an account of his life and thoughts.

It would, of course, be easy to make a figure of fun out of Margery, who so frankly reveals herself. Even so sympathetic a writer as Father Herbert Thurston speaks of her 'terrible hysteria', while Miss Hope Allen says: 'she was petty, neurotic, vain, illiterate, physically and nervously overstrained.' These things often betrayed her into outrageous and undignified behaviour, unworthy of herself or of her dedicated aims. The self-portrait of a minor mystic remains, however, the more credible for its merciless honesty and its fidelity to life.

Lynn in the fourteenth-century was a prosperous town with a flourishing trade with Scandinavia, Germany and the Low Countries. Its great church of St Margaret, the Guildhall and other buildings told of the wealth of its citizens who had contributed so handsomely to the funds for their construction. Among the leading citizens was John Burnham, the father of Margery, a man who had been elected mayor no less than five times and was for long an alderman of the borough. At one time he represented Lynn in Parliament, and was associated with the influential Corpus Christi Gild of the town. It was into this good bourgeois family that Margery was born about

1373, and about her twentieth year she was married to another *bon bourgeois*, John Kempe, a freeman of the borough, a member also of the Corpus Christi Gild, and soon after his marriage one of the borough chamberlains. More than that we know little of him and of the part he played in the municipal and commercial life of the town, although members of his family (and probably himself) were engaged in trade with various seaboard towns of Germany from time to time.

We may imagine, however, that on marrying John Kempe, Margery could look forward with confidence to the normal life of one of the town aristocracy, blessed with money and family connexions as she was. So far as her private life went, however, it opened badly, for her first-born caused her much suffering and illness—so much so, that, fearing she would not survive, and wishing to clear her conscience of a matter that had long been haunting her, she sent for her confessor and began to unburden herself. Before she had got very far, or had reached the principal matter that was troubling her, her confessor began to reprove her so sharply that she feared to go on and was silenced. Overwhelmed by her confessor's reproaches and burdened by a sense of guilt, her mind gave way, and for some seven months she was the victim of fears and hallucinations. At this time, she tells us, she saw, as she thought, devils open their mouths flaming with burning tongues of fire as if they would have swallowed her, sometimes ramping at her, sometimes threatening her, sometimes pulling and tugging at her both night and day. In her madness she slandered her husband and her friends, tried to destroy herself and lacerated her body with her nails, so that for a while she had to be bound and constantly watched. The day came, she believed, when sanity returned for, when she lay alone, Christ appeared to her in the likeness of a young man, clad in a mantle of blue silk, and sitting upon the bedside said: 'Daughter, why has thou forsaken Me, and I forsook thee never?' After this she recovered, and though her attendants remonstrated with him, her husband, 'having tenderness and compassion for her, commanded that they should deliver to her the keys', and she began to eat and to drink and her bodily strength returned.

Once she was recovered, she seems to have led a worldly life, and was notorious for the finery of her garments, cut in the latest fashion and made of brightly contrasting materials, so that men stared at her as she passed and her husband begged her to be more moderate. All in vain: she told him he should never have married above his station and that she would continue in her ways, hoping to outdo other wives in her array; she was for ever seeking the admiration and esteem of all beholders.

To increase her resources and to show that she was as good as another at practical affairs, she set up as a common brewer and for three or four years was one of the greatest brewers in the town. She was dogged with ill luck, however, and turned to milling. To this end she hired a man, and bought a pair of horses, and hoped with this horse-mill to make money, but here again she was unsuccessful: some said she was accursed and that it was God's vengeance on her, while others saw in it a call to her from worldly things to those of the spirit. Margery took the latter view, and henceforth her life was more and more given over to prayer and contemplation.

By this time some fifteen or sixteen years of married life had passed and many children had come, but henceforth Margery more and more longed for the celibate life. For a time, all her pleas to her husband were vain. He at least, had no such wish. The most he would say was that 'it were good to do so, but he might not yet. He would when God willed it.' In the meantime Margery increased her devotions. She would rise at two in the morning, go to church and stay there till noon or later. She fasted, wore a hair-cloth for mortification of the flesh, and ever prayed that a chaste life might soon be hers. At this time began that 'plentyous and continual weeping' that was to be with her for so many years, and which was to evoke such fierce and hostile criticism, for as she tells us: 'Many people thought that she could weep or leave off at will, and therefore called her a false hypocrite.'

Margery cared little then or later for such criticism. She went her own way, seeing visions, having rapturous communications with Christ: at times in great quiet of spirit, at others sunk in distress and despair. Temptations came, but were so easily repulsed that she fell into the sin of vainglory. Then to punish her, as it seemed, God tempted her with lecherous desires, to which in the end she was anxious to succumb, but was humiliated when she approached her would-be lover who now repudiated her, and said that he would never consent for all the gold in the world: 'he would rather be hewn as small as flesh for the pot.' Further tribulations of this kind assailed her, but after much prayer and meditation an end came to this period of trial in due course: she and her husband went from place to place for her soul's health, until on one of their journeys, as they came from York in very hot weather on Midsummer eve, the old question of marital chastity was raised between them and Margery declared that she would rather see her husband slain than yield again to him. Later, as they sat by a wayside cross on the way to Bridlington, they came to a final agreement that he should not come again to her bed, on condition that she should pay all his debts before she started on her projected pilgrimage to Jerusalem. They solemnized their agreement by saying three paternosters kneeling beneath a cross in a field, and then with great gladness of spirit ate of the cake carried in his bosom and drank the beer from the bottle in her hand. Her emancipation was complete: henceforth, her husband was but a secondary figure in her life. She was the spouse of Christ, and her every waking hour was only profitable if spent in his service.

As we have seen, the great pilgrimage to Jerusalem was already in her mind, but, before this could be arranged, she spent much time moving about the country, at times impressing people by her sincerity and devotion, but often she ran into trouble by her outspokenness and scorn of religious men. At Canterbury she was accused of being a Lollard and threatened with the stake; at other times it was said an evil spirit vexed her or that some bodily sickness occasioned her behaviour, for she was wont to fall down in convulsions, making wondrous faces and gestures, all the time sobbing bitterly and crying loudly. At this period of her life two desires were uppermost in her mind. First, she wished to take a formal vow of chastity before a bishop, and to receive the mantle and ring of widowhood as a sign of her new estate: and secondly, she desired to dress in white, as a sign of virtue and purity. To this end she went to Lincoln to ask Bishop Philip Repington to grant to her her wishes. After waiting three weeks for the bishop to return to his palace she was received by him, and gave him an account of her meditations and contemplations, which so impressed him that he advised her to have them written down. This she was unwilling to do, and twenty years were to pass before she felt the time was ripe for this. When she made her request to be professed with mantle and ring and given the white robe, the bishop took advice of his council, and endeavoured to put her off until she returned from Jerusalem when, he said, she would be 'better proved and known'. In so doing he displayed worldly prudence, for to have afforded official recognition to this eccentric woman might have given his enemies a handle against him. This decision did not suit Margery, and on the next day she

> went to church and prayed to God with all her spirit that she might have knowledge how she might be governed in this matter, and what answer she might give to the Bishop.
>
> Our Lord Jesus Christ answered to her mind in this manner:
>
> Daughter, say to the Bishop that he fears the shames of the world more than the perfect love of God.... Therefore, daughter, tell him though he will not do it now, it shall be done another time when God willeth.

The bishop apparently took no offence at this bold speech, but advised her to go to the archbishop of Canterbury 'and to pray him to grant leave to me, the bishop of Lincoln, to give her the mantle and the ring, since she was not of his diocese. This cause he feigned through counsel of his clerks, for they loved her not.' Margery refused his advice, but said she would go to the archbishop 'for other causes and matters which I have to show to his reverence'.

Even this ungracious answer failed to rouse Repington, who gave her a present of two marks (26*s.* 8*d.*) and asked her to pray for him.

Margery and her husband made their way to Lambeth Palace, and while waiting in the great hall heard the archbishop's clerks, squires and yeomen swearing and cursing among themselves. With characteristic lack of tact she rebuked them, whereupon a richly dressed woman turned on her with a fury of imprecations and concluded: 'I would thou wert in Smithfield, and I would carry a faggot to burn thee with. It is a pity that thou art alive!'

Then she was sent for by the archbishop, who kept her talking to him in his garden 'till stars appeared in the firmament'. Archbishop Arundel was a great prince of the Church and a relentless foe of Lollardy, and the fact that he talked so long with her and found no 'default in her' is the strongest possible evidence of the strength of her personality and the essential orthodoxy of her views. So impressed by her was Arundel that he suffered her to rebuke him for the behaviour of his servants, for whom she said 'ye shall answer, unless ye correct them, or else put them out of your service'. Arundel replied meekly and gave her a fair answer, and at length after much talk she came away.

As the autumn of the same year (1413) drew on Margery made the final preparations for her pilgrimage to the Holy Land. Her debts paid, she bade farewell to her husband and friends, and after praying at Norwich and again at Yarmouth, some time in November she sailed to the Netherlands and landed at Zealand. During the next month she and her companions travelled across Germany to Constance, and from there to Bologna, and so to

Venice which she reached in January 1414. Here began a tedious wait of some months before the time came for the pilgrim galleys to set out. In the meantime, however, Margery had encountered plenty of trouble. First, she was reproved because she would eat no flesh and cried so loudly and constantly as to make herself a nuisance. Besides they said that she would talk of nothing but the love of the Lord at all times and places. Her fellow-pilgrims roundly abused her, and told her that they would not put up with her as her husband did, while one of them went so far as to say: 'I pray God that the devil's death may overcome thee soon.' Some deserted her and induced her handmaiden to leave her, while a fellow-pilgrim who had charge of her money gave her only a fraction of it, and told her to fend for herself. Fortunately others were kinder and took her along with them, but at Constance her persecutors rounded on her again and cut her gown so short that it came but little below the knee, while at the same time they gave her a piece of white canvas cut in the shape of an apron so that she should be thought a fool and despised. They also made her sit at the end of the table below everyone else, where she dared not utter a word. An English friar took her part and set her on her way to Bologna with an old Devonshire man, William Weaver. There her former companions found her, and a reconciliation was effected, Margery promising not to speak of the Gospel in their presence, and to be merry when they sat at meat. On reaching Venice, however, they quarrelled again, and for weeks she was alone until the time came to sail, probably some time in April. Further trouble then arose, for her companions secretly hired gear and places for themselves in one ship and were reluctant to take her with them. They changed their minds, however, when they later discovered that her 'voices' had warned her not to sail in that ship and they incontinently left it, and much against her will all sailed with her in the ship of her choice —an unwilling tribute to the spiritual power she exerted.

Although Margery tells us nothing, we know much about these pilgrim convoys from other fifteenth-century writers who made the pilgrimage or who wrote manuals for travellers. One of the fullest accounts is given by Friar Felix Fabri, who made his second journey in 1484, some seventy years later than Margery, but in essentials the conditions had remained unchanged, and we may gather from his account a vivid picture of what it meant to sail in a pilgrim galley during the fifteenth century. As the spring advanced, a number of galleys began to make ready for the voyage, and the first thing to do was to bargain for a place on one of these. Although they were private ventures, the Venetian State exercised a strict control over their masters, and saw to it that reasonable living conditions were provided for the pilgrims while at sea, and that the masters were responsible for their safe-conduct in the Holy Land itself. 'Venetian galleys are as like one to another as swallows' nests', we are told, and the pilgrims found on going on board that their quarters were in a 'cabin' below deck, which stretched the whole length of the ship, and was 'like a great and spacious chamber'. The friar tells us that 'the berths of the pilgrims are so arranged that all along the ship, or rather the cabin, one berth joins the next one without any space left between them, and one pilgrim lies by the side of another along both sides of the ship, having their heads towards the side of the ship, and their feet stretching out towards one another. As the cabin is wide, there stand along the middle of it, chests and trunks in which the pilgrims keep their own private property.' Once the pilgrim had struck his bargain with the master, he was allotted his place, according to what he had paid, and throughout the voyage made himself comfortable there as best he could.

Before embarking, however, he had to provide himself with a variety of articles necessary for his journey. He was advised to buy 'a little caldron, a frying-pan, dishes, plates, saucers, cups of glass, a grater for bread and such necessaries'. A chest to hold his clothes and barrels for water and wine were essentials, while many took coops of hens and a variety of victuals, for though the captain contracted to feed them throughout their journey, 'some time ye shall have feeble bread and feeble wine and stinking water, so that many times ye will be right fain to eat of your own'. Furthermore, a mattress and bedding were essential, for the captain provided nothing of this kind.

Once the journey had begun, the pilgrims settled down to the tedium of the voyage, which lasted about a month, depending on the number of places called at *en route* for fresh provisions, water and trading; on the delays caused by storms and by the appearance of pirates and other enemy vessels from time to time. These things enlivened the journey which otherwise passed slowly enough in talking, reading, praying or writing. Some meditated, others took violent exercise, climbing the rigging or lifting heavy weights. At times all seemed at peace one with another: at times quarrels and disputes broke out, making the galley like hell, says Friar Felix, with the sound and fury of men's cursing and blasphemies. And finally 'there is among all the occupations of the seafarers one which, albeit loathsome, is yet very common, daily and necessary —I mean the hunting and catching of lice and vermin. Unless a man spends several hours in this work when he is on a pilgrimage, he will have but unquiet slumbers.' Games of chance, gambling and wine-drinking helped the hours to pass for some, while they waited for the call of the trumpet, summoning them to meals. On hearing this, all rushed to secure a place at one of the tables, 'for he who comes late gets a bad seat'. The meal is quickly served—salad, meat and some form of cereal and cheese, washed down by copious draughts of wine and water. A few noble or distinguished pilgrims had their own mess, and paid the cooks extra to cook for them, and the friar remarks on the noise and ill temper that comes from the close, over-heated cooks' galley as men struggle at the crowded fire-places to contrive a little space for their own pots and pans.

At nightfall with everyone trying to get to bed in very cramped quarters, all is noise and confusion. Quarrels easily arise, as each pilgrim tries to keep or win back the little space allotted to him. Those who have drunk too much are a particular nuisance, while the snores, moans and coughing of others, and the movements of the sailors overhead, prevent sleep coming easily, particularly as the heat steadily mounts in the crowded space and the scamperings of rats and mice help to take away the pilgrims' rest. As if this were not enough, some come to bed late and keep others awake by their chatter and by their refusal to put out their candles. Missiles and entreaties fail to move them: they only shout the louder and begin a new quarrel.

By day life also has its difficulties: petty theft is rampant; moving about the ship requires care, for things fall from above on the unwary pilgrim, and to walk carelessly in certain places involves the risk of being pitched overboard. The sailors are no respecters of persons, and when at work will roughly push aside or knock down those who get in their way. Hats are quickly blown away, while it is only too easy to drop valuable things into the sea when standing at the side of the boat.

From time to time the galley would put into some port so that fresh water, bread and other supplies could be laid in, and also to allow the master and his crew to buy and to sell, for all of them were determined and experienced bargainers. The pilgrims would also land to replenish their own stores, to see the sights and to pray at shrines and churches until the trumpets warned them that the ship was about to sail and that they must return at once. So the days wore on until the Holy Land drew near, and from the look-out an eager watch was kept, while the more ardent pilgrims stood hour by hour straining to see the sacred land of their desire. As soon as it was dawn they rushed on deck, and at last the watchman gave the long-expected signal, and gradually more and more of the pilgrims could see the land as the galley drew nearer, until at last it came to its anchorage in the harbour of Jaffa.

Now began a tedious wait for the pilgrims, anxious as they were to get on their way to Jerusalem, for they could not land until a safe-conduct had been received from the various Moslem officials who were the officers of the Mameluke sultans of Egypt. The master had first to get word sent to the governors of Jerusalem and of the other towns they would pass through for permission to proceed, and not until they had struck their bargains with the master was a single pilgrim safe to land. When finally they did so, they were herded like animals before the officials who entered their names on the roll, after which they were hustled along by Saracens into a series of caves, known as St Peter's cellars. Here the Christian dogs were roughly treated by their guards, who forbade them to wander outside although the caves were stinking with filth which lapped about their feet, and which they had to clear as best they could to make any space whereon they could lie. Their sufferings were eased by the arrival of traders who brought rushes and branches of trees which they placed on the miry ground while others brought sweet-smelling herbs, unguents and perfumes to solace the pilgrims. Others again brought bread and eggs, water, fruit and salads which they willingly bought, and afterwards settled down to rest, but not before a fierce looking Saracen had exacted a penny from each of them in the way of rent—an operation he repeated early the next morning before he would allow anyone to leave the cave. Throughout the day young Turkish men moved in and out, provoking the pilgrims by their insults and outrageous behaviour, and if they struck back haling them before the Turkish officials so that they might be fined.

No term could be fixed to these delays: they were at the mercy of the various overlords, and until these were satisfied they were cooped up like beasts in the caves. At last, however, the period of waiting was over. The convoy was formed, and mounted on asses, with an escort of Saracens, the captains and governors leading the way, the pilgrims set out for Jerusalem. Their journey was often an eventful one, for the countryside was full of Arabs watching for an opportunity to rob or pillage. They would fall upon any small group if unprotected, or would attach themselves to the caravan and steal scrips, clothes and the like if these fell to the ground or were left unguarded. As the pilgrims passed through the villages they were often met with curses or even with volleys of stones. In addition the cavalcade raised clouds of dust, and this and the great heat made nightfall and rest in one of the pilgrim houses particularly grateful. There they were able to buy food and drink from the villagers—bread, eggs, rice cooked in milk, fruit and wine—but had to be extremely careful not to provoke them in any way.

So they gradually made their way to Jerusalem: on viewing the city many of the pilgrims wept for joy, knelt and bowed their faces to the earth, and above all, says Friar Felix, 'the women pilgrims shrieked as though in labour, cried aloud and wept'. Within the city there was much to see, and all the many places associated with the sacred story were visited, culminating in the Church of the Holy Sepulchre, or the Temple as it was sometimes called. Here the pilgrims were shown the chamber in which was the supposed tomb of Christ, and in another part of the building was the hole that received the base of the Cross. Here also they spent the night in contemplation and prayer, Margery Kempe and her party staying within the Sepulchre from one evensong to the next.

On arrival in the Holy Land Margery's religious zeal and emotion knew no bounds. She could scarcely ride on her ass at times, so acutely did she feel, while Mount Calvary and other holy places provoked tremendous displays: she wept and sobbed plenteously; she fell down because she could not stand or kneel, and rolled and wrestled with her body, and cried as though her heart would burst asunder. This crying, indeed, became part of her for many years, for as she says:

> This manner of crying endured many years after this time for aught that any man might do, and therefore she suffered much despite and reproof. The crying was so loud and so wonderful that it astounded people unless they had heard it before, or unless they knew the cause of the crying. First she had her cryings at Jerusalem and also in Rome. And when she came home to England, they came once a month, then once a week, then daily, and once she had fourteen in a day! and so on as God would visit her. She never knew the time or the hour when they would come, and as soon as she found that she would cry, she would suppress it as much as possible so as not to annoy people. For some said it was a wicked spirit vexed her: some said it was a sickness: some said she had drunk too much wine: some wished she had been in the haven: some would she had been at sea in a bottomless boat: and thus each man had his own thoughts.

Obviously, Margery was not easy to live with, and the pilgrims again deserted her on their return to Venice, some of them saying that they would go with her no further for a hundred pounds. The Lord told her to go to Rome, whither she was led by a broken-backed, poverty-stricken man, Richard of Ireland, and finally she reached Rome about September 1414 and was there until the following spring. While there, she assumed the white habit she had so long desired to wear, and lived as best she could, since she gave away all her money at one point in obedience to the Lord's command. Richard, not unnaturally, was 'greatly moved and evil pleased because of this, and spake right sharply to her', but she pacified him, and went about serving the people, declaring the faith, begging from door to door, welcomed here and repulsed there as the event fell. She gives many examples of all this, and was sustained throughout by her constant communings and messages from the Lord, and finally at Easter 1415 set off for England. Despite fears of thieves assailing her and her party on the way, she reached Middelburg in Zealand by mid-May, and crossed over to England safely in a little boat in less than two days. She knelt and kissed the land on coming on shore, and happily passed on to offer the three-halfpence given to her then at the cathedral at Norwich.

So ended her first and greatest pilgrimage. She had been absent from England some eighteen months and had survived difficulties and dangers which would have overwhelmed one less convinced of her divinely controlled life. The habit of appealing to God for guidance grew on her, and she seldom seems to have failed to receive divine help, according to her own account. This made her more and more assured, and more and more difficult to live with. On her return she found a benefactor who furnished her with a new set of white robes, and these and her boisterous cries drew everyone's attention to her. 'Many said that there was never a saint in Heaven that cried as much as she did, and therefore they would conclude that she had a devil within her....And yet Our Lord made some to love her and cherish her, and have her home to meat and drink, and they had great gladness to hear her talk of Our Lord.'

How she lived after her return is unknown. She tells us she had no money and many debts, and must have relied on casual gifts and food from the devout who believed her to be inspired of God. For her own part she never doubted this was so, and two years after her return started off on another pilgrimage, despite her poverty, for she had been told: 'Daughter, study not for any money, for I shall provide for thee.' This time her ambition was to reach the great shrine of St James, at Compostella, in Coruña, Spain, where the saint's supposed remains were enshrined. To begin with she went across England to Bristol where she tells us she met by agreement the broken-backed man to whom she repaid money borrowed from him in Rome two years before! She could not sail at once, for all the available ships had been commandeered for the king's service to transport troops for the great invasion of France that summer. While waiting, her tears and sobs and cries and shrieks caused the usual differences of opinion among those who heard them and it was not surprising that the newcomer with her white habit and strange ways should have been summoned before the bishop of Worcester whose residence was just outside Bristol. Here occurred one of those incidents which made her notorious—an incident similar to that at Lambeth.

> When she came into the hall, she saw many of the Bishop's men in clothes freakishly cut in the fashion of the day. She lifting up her hands, blessed herself. And then they said to her: 'What devil aileth thee?' She said again: 'Whose men be ye?' They answered back: 'The Bishop's men.' And then she said: 'Nay, forsooth, ye are more like the Devil's men.' Then they were angry and chid her, and spoke angrily to her.

The bishop, however, received her kindly, saying that he knew her by repute, shrived and blessed her, and sent her on her way with money in her purse.

At last she sailed, but before doing so her fellow-pilgrims told her that if they met with tempests it would be because of her, and they would throw her in the sea. She survived, however; the outward journey taking seven days and the return, five. For the whole of a fortnight she was at the shrine, but tells us no more than that besides her 'great cries' and 'plenteous tears of compassion', she had 'great cheer, both bodily and of the spirit'.

Throughout this period the fear of Lollardy was strong in England. The arch-heretic, Sir John Oldcastle, was still at large in the summer of 1417 when Margery returned, and it was not until late November that he was captured, brought to London and burnt in mid-December. Characters such as Margery, with her strong individualism and outspoken condemnation of many ecclesiastics, inevitably fell under suspicion, and she was constantly in danger. Several times in the autumn of 1417 she was held to question, first at Leicester, on her way home from Bristol. There the mayor was strongly suspicious of her, and did not hesitate to call her 'a false strumpet, a false Lollard, and a false deceiver of the people'. He threatened to throw her into the common jail among a mass of men prisoners, but she was saved by the jailer who went surety for her and kept her in his own house. This did not protect her from the steward of Leicester, 'a seemly man', who took her into his chamber and made advances to her, but was abashed by her determined resolution. Later, she was brought before the abbot of Leicester and quickly persuaded him of her orthodoxy, but the mayor still remained unconvinced, and ordered her to go to the bishop of Lincoln and to bring back a letter discharging the mayor of all responsibility. This she did, and so after a three-week hold-up was able to go on her way.

She ran into more trouble in York, and finally was

brought before the archbishop at his palace of Cawood. Here she showed great courage (and rashness) in her replies to the archbishop, despite the fact that she 'trembled and shook', so that she hid her hands under her clothes, in order that this should not be noticed. First the archbishop asked her if she was a maid, since she was clothed in white, and sent for fetters, calling her a false heretic. When the archbishop took his seat she burst into tears. 'Why weepest thou, woman?' said the archbishop, to which she made the spirited reply: 'Sir, ye shall wish some day that ye had wept as sore as I.'

After questioning her on the Articles of the Faith, and finding nothing wrong, the archbishop said to her: 'I am evil informed of thee. I hear it said that thou art a right wicked woman.' And she answered back: 'I also hear it said that ye are a wicked man. And if ye be as wicked as men say, ye shall never come to Heaven, unless ye amend whilst ye be here.' Then said he very violently: 'Why, thou wretch, what say men of me?' She answered: 'Other men, sir, can tell you well enough.' Then said a great clerk with a furred hood: 'Peace! Speak of thyself, and let him be.' Afterwards the archbishop said to her: 'Lay thy hand on the book here before me and swear that thou shalt go out of my diocese as soon as you may.' This she refused to do till she had taken leave of friends, and visited her confessor at Bridlington. Then said the archbishop to her. 'Thou shalt swear that thou wilt neither teach nor reprove the people in my diocese.' 'Nay, sir, I shall not swear', she said, 'for I shall speak of God and rebuke those that swear great oaths wherever I go.' Replies such as these continued, until at last the archbishop called for a man to lead her away from him. The man asked for a noble (6*s.* 8*d.*) for his pains, but the archbishop would not pay so much. 'See, here is five shillings, and lead her rapidly out of this country', he said, and so ended this memorable interview.

Even now she was not finished with the archbishop, for on the way to Hull to cross the Humber into her own county, she was arrested by two officers of the duke of Bedford, who said their lord had sent for her as the greatest Lollard in all the country, and that they would have a hundred pounds for her arrest. So they conducted her to Beverley, and once again she faced the archbishop who was there with 'many great clerks, priests, canons and other men'. 'What, woman! art thou come again? I would fain be delivered of thee' was his exclamation on seeing her. Various new charges were brought against her, including one saying that she carried about letters on behalf of Sir John Oldcastle, but the archbishop was convinced that there was no substance in them, and finally granted her petition, and gave her a letter certifying her orthodoxy, and so at last she came back to Lynn, where 'a reckless man, little caring for his own shame, with will and of set purpose, cast a bowlful of water on her head as she came along the street'. Margery was home again!

The next fifteen years or so of her life seem to have been spent mainly at Lynn, and Margery gives a somewhat confused account of her many experiences at the hands of religious and secular folk. Her cries remained both her glory and her shame. Some thought them evidence of 'a right gracious gift of God', while others said that she had a devil in her. One of the most famous preachers in England, a grey friar, came to the convent at Lynn and endured patiently Margery's cries at his first sermon, but on a second occasion, her outburst caused him to say: 'I would this woman were out of the church, for she annoys the people', and although her friends said that she could not help it, he insisted that she must stay away, or be quiet. Despite all their pleas, he insisted on her absence, going so far as to bang his hand on the pulpit, saying: 'If I hear any more of these pleas, I shall so smite the nail on the head that it will shame all her supporters.' A number of years later her cries ceased, and 'as some spoke evil of her before when she cried, so now some spoke evil of her because she cried not'. Cries or no cries, she was well known to all in Lynn, and to many from outside, and from time to time was summoned to converse with learned doctors of theology and preachers of renown. Evidently by this time she had won a reputation for herself as one touched with the divine, and in moments of stress was appealed to for help. Thus in January 1421 there was a great fire in Lynn, and people were fearful lest the great church of St Margaret should be destroyed. Margery was encouraged 'to cry and weep as much as ever she would' in the hope that the Lord would show mercy; she advised the parish priest to bear the Sacrament as near the fire as he could to arrest its spread. This he did, while Margery prayed in the church, although the sparks were falling about her, until men with snow on their clothes came in to tell her that God had sent 'a fair snow to quench the fire with'. On another occasion a man implored her aid, since his wife was out of her mind from childbirth. 'And dame', he said, 'she knoweth not me, nor any of her neighbours. She roareth and cryeth so that she makes evil folk afeared. She will both smite and bite, and therefore she is manacled on her wrists.' Margery visited her, and by her kindness won her confidence, and in due time she was cured. 'It was, as they thought who knew of it, a very great miracle, for he that wrote this book had never before that time seen man or woman, as he thought, so far out of herself as this woman was, nor so evil to rule or to manage.'

Margery lived through these years, now up, now down: sustained by her constant divine guidance and messages, comforted by the conversation and reading of other mystics' writings by her learned friends, and from time to time vouchsafed visions of Christ's life and of his Passion which brought forth floods of tears and gave her much comfort.

Sometime St Peter, or St Paul; sometime St Mary Magdalen, St Katharine, St Margaret, or whatever saint in heaven she thought of, through the will and sufferance of God spoke to the understanding of her soul, and informed her how she should love God, and how she should best please him, and answered to whatever she would ask of them, and she could understand by their manner of converse which of them it was that spoke to her and comforted her. Our Lord of his mercy, visited her so often and so copiously with his holy conversation that frequently she was unaware of how the day had passed. It was so sweet and so devout that it fared as if she had been in Heaven.

Her active days were not quite over, for when she was about sixty years old, in 1433, she set out on her last adventure. It happened that one of her sons had married a German woman, and brought her and his daughter to visit his mother at Lynn, and died there shortly after. The wife remained with Margery for eighteen months, and then wished to go home to Prussia, and Margery decided to go as far as Ipswich with her to see her safely embarked. *En route*, the voice of the Lord commanded her to go overseas with her daughter-in-law, and so she embarked, despite her daughter-in-law's entreaties to her not to do so. They encountered violent storms, and were forced to land on the Norway coast, but some weeks later were able to sail and arrived in Danzig late in April. She had set forth entirely unprepared, and was grateful to the master of the ship who gave her warm clothing and showed her much kindness.

After some weeks in Danzig, Our Lord admonished her to depart. This made her very uneasy, for she feared the sea and there was war in the country through which she must pass. Providentially, a man met with her and asked if she would go on pilgrimage with him to the Holy Blood at Wilsnak, in Brandenburg. To this she agreed, and after various difficulties they went by sea to Stralsund in Pomerania, and then by land. She soon fell out with her companion, who was fearful of being found in company with an Englishwoman, 'for there was open war betwixt the English and those countries' through which they passed. He also feared meeting with thieves, and pressed on at a great pace, much irritated by Margery's characteristic tears and sobbings. She collapsed at last, was brought into Wilsnak on a hay-wain, and from there was carried on in the same fashion towards Aachen; but after a while was deserted by her companion, and spent a miserable time until she joined a company of poor folk on their way to Aachen. She gives a vivid picture of their journey begging in each town, and

when they were without the towns, her fellowship took off their clothes, and sitting naked, picked themselves. Need compelled her to await for them and to prolong her journey.... She was afraid to put off her clothes as her fellows did, and therefore, through being with them, had part of their vermin, and was bitten and stung very evilly both day and night. She kept on with her fellowship with great anguish and discomfort and much delay, until they came to Aachen.

From there, after she had seen Our Lady's smock and other relics, her way to Calais was a series of misadventures. People promised to take her with them and then went off without her: others said she could go with them so long as she could keep up, and when she failed to do so, left her. Lodging was hard to come by, and companions few and often untrustworthy. She made the last stages with a poor friar, and together they struggled on, until wellnigh exhausted they arrived at Calais, where she paid the friar what little she had for his help, and sought out friends in the town.

Fortune favoured her, and she received food and lodging, fresh clothing and much kindness from them, but was cold-shouldered by fellow-pilgrims waiting to sail, who obviously did not want her with them (what the cause, she never knew) and would give her no information. However, after four days, she got a place on a boat, and by divine intervention was protected from sea-sickness and was able to care for a woman who had been particularly unkind to her.

At Dover they all left her, and 'therefore she took her way Canterbury-ward by herself alone, sorry and sad in manner that she had no fellowship and that she knew not the way'. From there she came to London, 'clad in a cloth of canvas, as it were a sacken apron', thus drawing much attention and derision upon herself. Many priests would not have her in their churches, and many jokes and stories were told against her. She gave as good as she received and 'spoke boldly and mightily wheresoever she went in London, against swearers, cursers, liars, and such other vicious people, against the pompous array, both of men and women. She spared them not, she flattered them not, either for their gifts, or for their meat, or for their drink.'

From here she went to Richmond to worship at the Brigittine house called Syon Abbey, and there on Lammas Day (1 August) saw the hermit who had accompanied her and her daughter-in-law to Ipswich the previous year. She begged him to lead her back to Lynn, saying, 'Ah, Reynald, you are welcome. I trust our Lord sent you hither, for now I hope as you led me out of Lynn you shall bring me home again.' The hermit was very unwilling, but at last consented, and so she came again to Lynn.

Towards the end of her days she made two attempts to record all that had happened in her adventurous life. Although she had often been asked to put it down on paper, she for long refused, saying that the time was not ripe. Shortly before her last journey, however, she decided that the time had now come and, as she thought, the man to act as her amanuensis, for she could not write herself. This man, she tells us, had lived for many years in 'Dutchland' (Germany), and on his return had come to live with her. Although she does not say so, it seems highly probable that this was her son, who, as we have seen, came to Lynn with his wife and child about this time. Be this as it may, he had only taken down part of her story when he died, and for a while Margery could get no one to help her. In the end she prevailed on a priest whom she trusted, and who had pressed her to set down her story, to look at what had been done. When he did so he complained that the language was neither English nor 'Dutch', and furthermore that the book was written in a difficult hand which he was most reluctant to try to reduce to order. Finally he made a start in July 1435, and although he found the script so hard to read that he thought the Devil had affected his eyesight, by reading it word by word to Margery and being aided by her memory when the text was obscure, he successfully re-wrote Book I, and then turned to write Book II, telling of Margery's further history and her last pilgrimage. This second book he began on 28 April 1438. While the book in its outlines gives a true account of Margery's life it makes no claim to chronological exactitude, for many years had passed since the events described occurred. Nevertheless, wherever people or events are mentioned which can be exactly placed, it is remarkable how accurate her memory appears to have been.

Once all this was safely set down Margery's eventful career was nearing its end. At any rate we hear no more of her, and can leave her in her native place, happy among religious buildings that had meant so much to her, and sustained by the certainty and faith that had carried her through so many adventures over the years.

RICHARD BRADWATER

'THE short and simple annals of the poor' were no more plentiful or easy to interpret in the Middle Ages than they were in Gray's time. Yet when we remember that it has been estimated that there were fifteen countrymen to every townsman in the fifteenth century, and that the majority of these countrymen were but poor villagers, it is obvious that difficult or easy, no picture of medieval life could be satisfactory that ignored this great body of men and women, whose lives were obscure, but whose labours were an essential element in the agricultural economy—an economy, be it remembered, that was the principal factor in providing both the money and produce on which lords and landowners of whatever degree mainly depended. On many thousands of manors up and down the country there was a great body of men and women, some well off, some miserably poor, continuously employed in winning a living for their lords and themselves from the soil. One such poor family was observed with a sympathetic eye by a contemporary, who tells us how as he went on his way he saw a poor man hanging on to his plough. His coat was of a poor stuff called 'cary'; his hood was full of holes and his hair stuck out of it. As he trod the soil his toes stuck out of his worn and thick-soled shoes; his hose hung about his hocks and he was beslobbered with mud from following the plough. His two mittens, scantily made of rough stuff, with worn-out fingers, were stiff with muck. Bemired with mud, almost up to his ankles, he drove four heifers before him that had become so feeble that men might count every rib, so sorry looking they were.

Beside him walked his wife, carrying a long goad, her short dress tucked up high, with a winnowing-sheet round her as a protection against the cold weather. She was barefoot, so that the ice cut into her feet and made them bleed. At the end of the row was a little wooden bread-bowl which held a small child covered with rags and on one side of it stood the two-year old twins. They all sang one song that was pitiful to hear: they all cried the same cry—a note full of care. The poor man sighed deeply and said, 'Children, be still!'

Even Langland could not surpass this vivid picture, although he often wrote of the hard lot of 'women that wonieth in cotes', and paused to describe the difficulties the peasant had in making ends meet with little else than loaves of bran and of beans, new cheeses, a few vegetables and the like to see him through until harvest time. A failure of his crops, or the destruction of his livestock by the murrain, left him in a desperate condition and an easy victim to plague and disease.

A wholly black picture, however, would be clearly false. The villager of the fifteenth-century had also his pleasures and his days of sober content. The feasting and festivities at Christmas and other festivals were red-letter days. Work was suspended: often he ate hugely up at the hall at the lord's expense, and contentedly watched the antics of the mummers, or gambolled around in the carols —part song, part dance—or bemusedly beat the table with his horn or pewter mug as he sang:

> Back and side, go bare, go bare,
> Both hand and foot go cold,
> But belly, God send thee good ale enough,
> Whether it be new or old!

Ale, indeed, was a word of might. Scot ale, church ale, wake ale, bride ale, Whitsun ale—a whole variety of names cloak so many excuses for merry-making and heavy drinking. More justifiable were the rejoicings of periods of the agricultural season—Plough Monday, midsummer eve, the conclusion of the hay or the corn harvest, when at times the lord would give a sheep or a ram for the feast and ale flowed freely at call.

The peasant's ordinary days, however, were spent in steady labour on his own lands and on those of his lord. The rhythm of the seasons held him in thrall. Ceaselessly he laboured; preparing, planting, tending, reaping—round and round he went with the passage of the months. He might hold more or less land than his neighbour, or might escape this or that service which fell on his friend, but the majority of men in the village felt themselves part of a community. Life was hard for all, but they shared much in common—both in rewards and in duties. Unless they had the misfortune to serve a harsh lord, or to run into a spell of illness or other trouble, life was endurable—at times perhaps more than that. Let us look at things as they were on one manor early in the fifteenth century.

The manor of Tooting-Bec in the county of Surrey was one of many which had belonged for generations to the

Abbey of Bec-Hellouin in Normandy, and about 1394 was leased to the priory and convent of Merton, who held their first manor court at Tooting on 13 December 1394. From then onwards, we can follow the fortunes of the manor for some decades, and may well begin with the first court of Dom Michael Kempton, prior of Merton, held on 18 October 1403. The place of the prior appears to have been filled by Dom John Schaldebourne, the cellarer, for this was one of the manors allocated to him, and from which he drew part of the funds necessary for the support of his office which was charged with providing the convent's supplies of liquor.

Before he entered and took his seat in the court, much had to be done. In the first place the courtroom had to be cleaned, beds prepared and rushes strewn on the floors of the rooms to be occupied by the cellarer and his staff. These great ones of Holy Church were not easily satisfied and the manorial officials had good reason to see that everything was well if they wished to escape rebuke. While all was being prepared, the bailiff or his subordinate would go from house to house, summoning the tenants to appear early the next morning at the court; and since it was no ordinary court, but a Leet court, at which all males over twelve years of age were bound to attend, he reminded householders to bring their sons and others with them.

On the morning itself, the tenants (or suitors as they were called) appeared at the manor court, and stood around on the rush-strewn floor of the court room. The various manorial officials—the hayward, the ale-tasters, the bailiffs and the tithing-men—also took their places, and with the cry of 'Silence!' echoing through the hall, the cellarer entered, and sat at the table on the dais, his clerk at his side. The clerk carried the bulky court roll, on which the proceedings of earlier courts were written, and unrolling it, began to write, in Latin: 'The first court of Dom Michael of Kempton, Prior of Merton, held there with view [of frank pledge] on the 18th day of the month of October in the beginning of the fifth year of the reign of King Henry the Fourth after the Conquest, John Schaldebourne being Cellarer.'

A threefold 'Oyez' from the bailiff in the meanwhile was followed by the order that all those who owed suit and service to the lord prior of Merton should draw near. The court was in session. Since it was the first court of the new prior, the first business was the swearing of fealty by the tenants present. Twenty of them, including three women one by one came forward and, placing their right hand on the Gospels, repeated after the cellarer: 'I will be toward my lord prior true and faithful, and bear to him fealty and faith for the lands and tenements which I hold of him, and I will truly do and perform the customs and services that I ought to do: so help me God.' After kissing the book each retired, and so the ceremony went on, till all had sworn and the ordinary business of the court could begin. First of all came the essoins or excuses for non-attendance. Sickness, absence on the king's business or on pilgrimage, difficulties of travel because of floods or of enemies were accepted as valid pleas by the cellarer, and the friends of the absentees pledged themselves to produce them at the next court. The clerk noted all these names on his rolls, and then the ordinary pleas were heard. These were of many kinds, but fell into well-defined groups. Often a holding had become vacant by death, or because the holder was too weak to carry out his duties and to keep his land in proper condition. This was reported by the bailiff, and if he was in court, the tenant surrendered the land into the cellarer's hands. Whereupon one of his relatives would ask to be allowed to take on the holding, and generally this was permitted, on payment of a fine for entry, and on swearing fealty. Then as a sign of his admission to the holding the cellarer handed to the man a white rod, and the ceremony was finished. All in court had seen what happened; all had heard their neighbour swear fealty and listened to the terms on which he took up the holding. Both Lord and man were protected by this public act, which for further security was inscribed on the court rolls, and could be (and was) appealed to if a difference of opinion arose.

After such matters were disposed of (and they did not arise at every court), more day-to-day items were considered. Offences against the manorial economy, such as putting too many beasts on the common, or failure to repair a dilapidated tenement or a broken pathway, or to clean a ditch so that the highway was flooded, were punished by a small fine, usually the equivalent of the wages for one or two days' work. Failure to report to the bailiff on the days when the lord's fields were cultivated by the labour of the tenants, or slackness at work, or late coming, or impudence to the officials also called for a fine. Quarrels between the tenants were heard, and if necessary adjourned for witnesses to support what had been said. Then when all had been heard, the court gave judgement and a fine was exacted from the guilty party. Since so much of the lives of these people was passed in communal activities, either in working on the lord's lands or in cultivating the great common-fields which they shared among them, it was important that matters of dispute should be settled as quickly and as finally as possible. The manor court afforded an opportunity for this. Then when these matters were settled more personal problems were heard. Leave to live off the manor had to be obtained formally, for every able-bodied man was of interest to the lord, since it was in part by his labour and payments that the lord existed. If a young man wished to go to the neighbouring grammar school with a view to becoming a priest in due time, or if he wished to go to work elsewhere leave had to be sought, and a fine for permission paid. If a girl married outside the manor a similar transaction took place, for in releasing her the lord forfeited the potential services and payments of any children she might bear. Should anyone leave the manor without permission, the tenants were ordered to produce him at the next court. This they seldom did, and at times were fined for not doing so, but the fugitive's name was entered court after court as a reminder.

The lord's material interest in his serfs was most strikingly shown in his attitude to offences against morality. If a man was convicted of adultery in the ecclesiastical courts and was fined, he lost something which was theoretically his lord's. Similarly a woman who lost her virginity had lost something of value, and was finable for depreciating her lord's property.

Then again, all acts of violence were matters which concerned the court. Brawling, fighting, assaults on manorial officials or tenants, driving off a neighbour's cattle, breaking the hedges of his close, carrying off his crops or by force releasing animals from the village pound—these and other offences against the peace of the village were heard and summarily punished by the lord.

Let us come a little closer to these people by following for a few years the fortunes of one of them, so far as we can discern anything about so unimportant a man who lived over five centuries ago. Among the peasants waiting outside the court-house on 18 October 1403 was Richard Bradwater, well known to his fellows as a domineering, law-breaking man, and one whose activities constantly brought him into conflict with the authorities and with his fellows. Like others, he had come to swear fealty to the new prior, for he was one of the largest holders of land on the manor. In his own name he held a cottage and 13½ acres of land, scattered about in the fields cultivated in common by all the peasants. For all this he paid an annual rent of twelve pence, but in addition gave to the lord what was perhaps even more valuable—labour services of various kinds. His forebears had given even greater services, but now he made a yearly payment of two shillings for permission not to do certain works. Even so, every year he was bound to mow one acre, three roods, of the lord's meadow, on which occasion the lord provided him with breakfast on the first day—probably a meal of rye-bread with beer and cheese. Later in the year he had to go himself, or to send a substitute, to reap for eight days at the corn harvest, when twice a day, at dinner and supper, he ate at the lord's expense. On such occasions nothing elaborate was provided—a thick soup or pease-porridge, bread and cheese, with an onion to flavour them; herrings or dried fish for fast days, and a piece of meat from time to time. These were washed down by draughts of a thin ale or by cider, and were all the reward he got for his labour, save that perhaps at Tooting as on some manors, towards the end of the mowing the lord released a sheep into the field, which served as a feast for the tenants if they could catch it. At other places also, the tenants were allowed to carry home as much hay or straw as they could bind in a single bundle upon their sickle or scythe handle, so long as the handle did not touch the ground; or as much hay as the hayward could lift with his little finger as high as his knee. Despite these small alleviations, however, Bradwater and his friends found these works a burden, and from time to time came late or not at all when they should have done, or failed to work to the satisfaction of the officials. These offences, as we have seen, were reported at the next manor court and fines imposed.

In addition to these harvest duties, Bradwater had also to perform other agricultural works from time to time—weeding, ploughing and harrowing. For these he got no food, and if he had no horse, then he was made to do some other work. If he shared a horse with another man then they did the ploughing or harrowing together. Apart from the harvesting, therefore, we see that Bradwater was not overburdened with his lord's affairs: the week in, week out day-works required of his ancestors were a thing of the past, and now most of his time was his own. The only other annual payment was a trivial one of a cock and a hen, provided once a year on St Thomas's Day (21 December).

One other payment was exacted from Bradwater and all his fellow-holders, namely a heriot at their death. This meant that at such a moment, the lord had the right to claim the best beast in the dead man's possession. Recently Bradwater could remember how the lord had claimed as a heriot the cow of William Hauldrone, valued at 11*s.*, and a sheep worth 2*s.*, belonging to his relative William Bradwater.

In addition to his own land, he also held till the coming of age of his nephew a little house and enclosure, together with nine acres, and for this he had to pay 3*s.* 6*d.* a year, and to send a man to help get in the lord's hay and grain for one day each year.

In all these things Bradwater's holdings and services were similar to those of the nineteen other men and women who did fealty that day. Few of them, however, were as objectionable to their neighbours as he was, and every court saw him in trouble. As soon as all present had sworn fealty Richard stepped forward and asked the cellarer's leave to come to an agreement with his neighbour John Yuery. At the previous court in April, John had complained that Bradwater had broken his covenant concerning the ploughing of an acre. Men often pooled their resources to help make up a plough-team, and evidently Bradwater had not appeared as he had promised to do and John Yuery said he was 2*s.* the poorer because of this. Bradwater partially admitted the offence, and asked that the damage should be assessed by his fellow-holders, or the homage as they were called. Such an inquiry enabled the cellarer to know whether John Yuery's claim was excessive or no. The homage were ordered to report at the October court, but in the meantime Bradwater had evidently come to an agreement with Yuery. The court accepted this arrangement and Bradwater paid a fine of 2*d.* and the cellarer passed on to the next item, and again the same two men were concerned—this time over the trespass of Bradwater's beasts in Yuery's wheat. When this accusation was made in April, Bradwater was told to bring five men at the next court who would swear with him that he had not committed the offence. Again Bradwater preferred to come to a private agreement and pay his twopenny fine. In yet a third claim made by Yuery of trespass in his grass, Bradwater found it best to be conciliatory. Things did not go so easily for him when he had to admit that his beasts had been in the prior's meadow, and he was fined the considerable sum of 6*s.* 8*d.*, and a further 6*d.* for his horses being found among the prior's oats.

After a few more cases had been heard, Bradwater's name was mentioned again, for John Pykestone complained that Bradwater's pigs had got into his close and had committed damage which he estimated at 3*s.* 4*d.* Bradwater could not wholly deny the charge, and asked that it should be assessed by the homage. This was done at once, and they declared that Pykestone had suffered damages to the extent of 3*s.* This Bradwater was ordered to pay before the next court, his goods and chattels to be forfeit if necessary.

Now it was Bradwater's turn, for he brought no less than seven charges against Pykestone, whom he accused of allowing his beasts to make havoc of Bradwater's oats, barley and wheat. He also accused Pykestone of killing a lamb and also some of his pigs and ducks. Most of the cases were stood over to the next court so that Pykestone could appear with three of his fellows ready to swear as to his innocence; while in one case Pykestone acknowledged himself to be at fault and the homage assessed the damage at 2½*d.* Bradwater had claimed 3*s.* 4*d.*! No further comment on Bradwater's actions is perhaps necessary, but we may note that when the time came for the rehearing of Bradwater's charges, Pykestone and his supporters appeared, and swore that the accusations were false. Bradwater was fined 1*s.* (2*d.* for each case) for wasting the time of the court. On the other hand, Pykestone made a number of new charges against Bradwater which he could not deny, and the homage found against him for various sums. He was fined a further 2*d.* for asserting that Robert Crafte had maimed his sow so that it lost its litter of nine piglets, to the damage of 10*s.* Robert asserted that he had made satisfaction and asked that the rolls of the court might be inspected to prove his words. This was done, and the entry was found—to Bradwater's discomfiture.

So we might go on from court to court, for there were few held at which he did not figure, and we can follow much of the manorial arrangements as we watch him breaking the laws of the manor, trespassing on his neighbour's land or despoiling their property. He is found putting more animals on the village common than he was entitled to do, or taking away his beasts from the pound wherein they have been enclosed by the village pounder because of some breach of the manorial regulations. He constantly encroached on his neighbours' holdings, thus reaping oats or cutting hay that was theirs, or causing trouble to others by failing to clean out his ditches. The bailiff accused him of stealing parts of a cart and also of assault on one occasion, and other tenants evidently found that he was no respecter of property and were constantly making accusations against him.

It would be possible to follow the activities of the other members of the manor as reflected in the Court Rolls, from which we should see even more clearly the communal life these medieval peasants lived. As is well known they all had holdings in the two or three great fields which surrounded their dwellings: holdings which were scattered in half-acre strips throughout the field, so that no one held any great area in one place. They were thus forced into close contact with one another, and a troublesome neighbour like Bradwater must have been a thorn in the flesh when the peasants were trying to arrange for communal ploughing or like activities, or when they were settling the details of each man's rights on the common, etc.

Not only their own interests but the prior's interests forced them to concern themselves one with another. The frankpledge or tithing system common at the time divided the tenants into groups (originally of ten), each group being responsible for the conduct and discipline of its individual members. Once a year the lord of the manor held his 'view of frankpledge', at which minor offences such as brewing without licence, assaults between neighbours, neglect of cleansing ditches and abuse of communal rights were dealt with. The tenant responsible for his group was known as the tithing man, and he reported cases such as the above, or told of boys who had now reached twelve years of age, or of newcomers to the manor who ought to be formally placed in his tithing. The members of the tithing were held responsible one for another to a considerable degree and could be fined for not reporting offences, or for neglecting to make inquiries as ordered by the court.

Furthermore, the necessity to render so many days' harvesting or ploughing postulated that all would do their part: a shirker or lazy worker put a strain on his fellows, as did a bad farmer who neglected his weeding or the keeping in control of his livestock. All had a part to play in the manorial economy, and for the most part they seem to have lived together composing their differences and working side by side without any appeal to the prior being necessary. A Bradwater was a nuisance, but fortunately there were not many Bradwaters, although Langland's lines on such men testify to their presence on some manors. 'If I went to the plough I pinched so narrowly that I would steal a foot of land or a furrow, or gnaw the half-acre of my neighbour; and if I reaped, I would over-reap [i.e. reach over into my neighbour's ground], or gave counsel to them that reaped to seize for me with their sickles that which I never sowed.'

Bradwater and his fellows, then, enable us to see something of what life was like on this manor in the early fifteenth century. As on thousands of other manors, its inhabitants were comparatively few: on the Tooting side there were only an average of ten in the tithing over some twenty-six years, and on the Streatham side the average was five. Assume the average medieval family was five (parents and three children), then Tooting accounted for fifty and Streatham for twenty-five inhabitants in the two parts of the manor. As we have seen, they held their land as did many others at this time by an arrangement with their lord whereby the actual physical services they were called on to perform were few, since they had bought their freedom from these by an annual payment. Such works as were left could not be considered onerous, and furthermore many servile 'incidents' were not in force, or had been abandoned by the lord. We find, for example, that sometimes no fine is exacted when a girl is married outside the manor, or if she has lessened her market value by being convicted of adultery. Permission to live outside the manor had to be obtained, but the annual fine was small. On the other hand the right of succession to a holding by the dead man's heirs was recognized. On the heir appearing in court he was given seisin of his father's lands, paying a fine on entry, and doing fealty to the lord. The men of Tooting were well on the way to complete personal freedom, and were already holding 'by copy of court roll' so that they were in the position described by Norden as 'tenants whom the favourable hand of time hath much enfranchised'. Within a brief space of time all servile bonds were to be removed and they were to begin a new life as free men.

NOTE ON SOURCES

A detailed bibliography of works on the historical, economic and social history of the years covered by the lives of the characters discussed in this volume will be found in my *Chaucer and the Fifteenth Century* (Oxford, 1947), pp. 240–63. For the lives and activities of my characters I have depended on original and secondary material as follows:

HUMPHREY, DUKE OF GLOUCESTER

The standard life of Humphrey is that of K. H. Vickers (1907), to which I am much indebted. It deals with all sides of his life and has an excellent bibliography. Earlier accounts, such as that of R. Pauli in his *Pictures of Old England* (1861), pp. 373–407, and the article by T. F. Tout in the *Dictionary of National Biography*, vol. XXVIII, may still usefully be consulted.

For his alliance with Jacqueline of Hainault see Ruth Putnam's *A Mediaeval Princess* (1904). Important material relative to his correspondence with Pier Candido Decembrio and others will be found in articles by M. Creighton, Mario Borsa and W. L. Newman in the *English Historical Review*, vols. X (1895), XIX (1904) and XX (1905) respectively. His gifts to the University of Oxford are recorded in *Munimenta Academica*, Rolls Series, 2 vols. (1868), and *Epistolae Academicae Oxon*, Oxford Historical Society, 2 vols. (1898).

Note on Sources

SIR JOHN FASTOLF

The best account of Sir John Fastolf's life and activities is that by Sir Sidney Lee in vol. XVIII of *D.N.B.* Fuller material on some points will be found in the authorities quoted at the end of the article, in particular *The Paston Letters* (ed. J. Gairdner, 6 vols., 1904); *History of Castle Combe* by Poulett Scrope (1852); *History of Caister Castle* by D. Turner (1842), and the various French and English chronicles mentioned by Sir Sidney Lee. The printed Calendars of the Close Rolls and the Patent Rolls for this period also yield some information.

THOMAS HOCCLEVE

His verse, with its revealing personal passages, will be found in three volumes of the Early English Text Society, extra series, vols. LXI (1892), LXXII (1897) and LXXIII (1925). The first of these contains a life of Hoccleve by F. J. Furnivall, and an appendix of documents from the Record Office. Some additional information has since come to light by the publication of several volumes of the Calendars of the Patent Rolls and of the Close Rolls, and from the article by H. C. Schulz in *Speculum*, vol. XII (1937), and in a letter of mine in the *Times Literary Supplement* of 1 January 1954 on the date of Hoccleve's death.

The organization and working of the Privy Seal have been fully investigated by T. F. Tout in his great work *Chapters in the Administrative History of Medieval England*, 6 vols. (1920–33).

Osbern Bokenham's *Legendys of Hooly Wummen* have been well edited by Mary S. Serjeantson for the E.E.T.S., original series, vol. CCVI (1936), while her Introduction gives the fullest account we have of the poet and his writings. Samuel Moore wrote two interesting articles on literary circles in East Anglia, entitled 'Patrons of Letters in Norfolk and Suffolk, *c.* 1450', which were printed in the *Publications of the Modern Language Association of America*, vols. XXVII and XXVIII (1912–13).

MARGARET PASTON

The correspondence of Margaret and other members of the Paston family has been edited with a most valuable Introduction by James Gairdner, the definitive edition in six volumes being published in 1904. An account of the family and their fortunes during the century, and of the material the letters provide will be found in my work, *The Pastons and their England* (1922). The day-to-day expenses of another squire's family mentioned above on p. 111 come from *The Household Book of Dame Alice de Bryene, 1412–13*, edited by V. B. Redstone (Suffolk Institute of Archaeology and Natural History, 1931).

MARGERY KEMPE

The text of Margery Kempe's biography was first published in 1936 by Colonel W. Butler-Bowdon in a modernized version for the ordinary reader. This was followed in 1939 by an edition for the E.E.T.S. by Professor S. B. Meech which printed the work in its original spelling and was embellished with an Introduction, and by very extensive notes by the editor and Miss Hope Emily Allen who first identified the manuscript. A second volume by Miss Allen, which will be in effect a study of mysticism in the fifteenth century, has been promised but has not yet appeared.

The notes and references are so full that they contain all the information the most avid reader could require. The references on pp. 288 ff. to the accounts of pilgrimages to the Holy Land are perhaps the most generally rewarding, to which may be added Miss H. F. M. Prescott's more recent recounting of some outstanding voyages in her *Jerusalem Journey* (1953), and the excellent chapter 'Pilgrimages' by P. S. Allen in *The Age of Erasmus* (1914).

Note on Sources

RICHARD BRADWATER

The day-to-day life of the peasant is described in detail in my *Life on the English Manor, 1150–1400* (1937), and in many respects it remained unchanged during the lifetime of Richard Bradwater. Professor R. H. Tawney in *The Agrarian Problem in the Sixteenth Century* (1912) discusses the changes that took place in the fifteenth century. The material from which this study was mainly compiled comes from *Court Rolls of Tooting-Bec Manor* (1909), edited by G. L. Gomme.

INDEX

Index

Index

Index

Index

Index

Index

Lightning Source UK Ltd.
Milton Keynes UK
UKOW03f1953040617
302625UK00001B/2/P